RILEY'S TREASURE CHASE

Best friends forever (photograph by Laurel Burke O'Connell)

RILEY'S
TREASURE CHASE

For young adults and their families

MICHAEL CLOHERTY O'CONNELL

with Riley

Two Lanterns illustration by Monica Vachula Paul Revere's Ride 2003

Hardcover ISBN: 979-8-9918207-3-8
Paperback ISBN: 979-8-9918207-4-5

Published by
One Then Two Lanterns LLC
11 LaMancha Way, Andover, MA 01810
Website & Blog: rileystreasurechase.com
mco@rileystreasurechase.com

Riley waiting for his Daddy to come home (photograph by Corey O'Connell)

This book was written in honor of Riley, our adorable sweet Cavapoo, and for every person who has earned the love of a dog, and knows their unconditional love, and great companionship. Riley loved children. This work is for their enjoyment, education, and adventure.

Though I hid over $100,000 in treasure in creating *Lady Liberty's Treasure Hunt* and *Riley's Treasure Chase* these chases or treasure hunts are not about seeking wealth. No one will get rich finding my treasures. The greatest treasure I can pass on here is to hope all of you have fun together on your adventures.

Riley was very patient traveling with me across all the towns, cities, trails, roads, and historical places outlined in this book. I've known the love of many dogs in my life but somehow Riley was my soul dog. I imagine when it is my time to cross over, that Riley and I will spend eternity together.

INTRODUCTION

This book is a Bay State (Massachusetts Colony circa 1770 - 1776) Treasure Hunt designed to teach children some important events that led to the birth of the United States of America as a nation. *Riley's Treasure Chase* is intended for parents and youth leaders to take young adults and their friends treasure hunting. Hopefully, during this fun adventure the children will develop a love for reading, history, fresh air, nature, hiking, and biking. Riley's Treasure Chase is devoted to today's and tomorrow's children, teaching them a bit about the American Revolution around Boston and its vicinity. May the light of *Liberty* burn bright in our children's, grandchildren's, and their grandchildren's hearts forever more.

BACKGROUND INFORMATION

Our family owns a wonderful Cavapoo dog named Riley. He is cute, cuddly, and is black, brown, and white – just plain adorable. With a last name like O'Connell, we had to give our sweet Cavapoo an Irish or Celtic first name.

Riley loves his family very much. His mommy, Laurel, buys him dog food and treats. He has stayed with his big sister Maryann at her house for weekends, hanging out while she works on her computer. He likes to go for walks with Brendan when he comes home from the Big Apple - New York City. Riley loves his brother Ryan, and they play ball all the time when Ryan comes home from the West Coast.

We call Ryan "the Dog Whisperer" because he loves dogs and seems able to actually communicate with them. Even difficult dogs love Ryan. That's pretty amazing.

Riley loves his brother Corey, too, because Corey takes him on boat rides on the Atlantic Ocean, pickup truck rides, and buys him fun toys all the time. Riley is a bit spoiled. He carries his toys around the house and gives them back to his buddy Corey. It's so cute and loving of Riley.

On a crisp November day in Boston, Riley jumped into my lap to warm up. I immediately snuggled him, giving him hugs and kisses. Riley loves the attention most of the time.

I am Riley's father, Michael, who he completely loves. Riley is so loyal. He sleeps by my side, or when he gets cold in the winter months, he climbs into my bed and under the blankets to warm up. Riley is a good boy but sometimes snores a little too much. I still love my little guy, even when he wakes me up from my sleep to go outside.

I carry Riley around, kiss him all the time, call him a baby, and spoil him. My family sometimes protests but Riley loves the attention. My children have all grown up, but Riley is always young at heart. His body may age but Riley's heart is forever young. His love is unconditional. That's why I named this chase after Riley so he will not be forgotten easily in our mortal world.

Riley loves car rides with his Mommy, Daddy and Corey. He puts his head out the passenger side window as the radio plays.

Riley on a happy car ride with Dad (photograph by Michael O'Connell)

He loves the fresh air blowing in his face. Corey and I like to take Riley through the drive-through at Dunkin' Donuts or to Donna's Donuts at 2106 Main Street, Tewksbury, MA. Riley is so cute and works his charm, so the staff always gives him treats. He loves that so much, and it's adorable. Please visit Donna's Donuts when you are following Tewksbury Minuteman Captain John Trull's trail, and tell them you know Riley dog from this book. You won't be disappointed. They are wonderful to their customers.

So Riley's Daddy, Michael, had a great idea. He decided to create a fun and cool treasure hunt so parents could go on fun trips with their children, get fresh air, learn some American history, and go treasure hunting together on weekends or vacation weeks.

It seemed like a fun project. The author also created and wrote a book for driving-age youth to adult's book called *Lady Liberty's Treasure Hunt*. The author decided this book was Parental Guidance for younger readers because there were some adult themes about loss in the book, and you need to drive a car to do *Lady Liberty's Treasure Hunt* effectively. You may read that book, and dream of *Lady Liberty's Treasure* under your parent's guidance.

Riley's father, Michael thought about this a longtime then decided this was not fair to younger adult readers; therefor he wrote this second book, and named it after Riley dog. Unfortunately there is some overlap in the two books but hopefully folks will understand that *Riley's Treasure Chase* was born from *Lady Liberty's Treasure Hunt.*

Adults, please let the children find *Riley's Treasure.* Don't steal their fun, glory, and personal growth by doing everything for them. Guide them gently with questions instead of doing too much for them. How great will it be for the young adult that finds the treasure with their own ideas and creativity, along with their loving parents' kind support to go on the quest.

I'm not sure yet which book will get released first, *Riley's Treasure Chase* or *Lady Liberty's Treasure Hunt.* Publishing books is complicated, that's for certain. I'm learning as I go. I guess that's part of life, regardless of how old we are. Continuous learning is the best path from age 9 to 99 or so. I may try to release the two books at once so your whole family can have a related treasure book and chase to enjoy.

Indiana Jones and the Last Crusade (Movie scene advertisement by Paramont Pictures)

Please remember to think like the treasure hunters in the famous movies: Raiders of the Lost Ark, Indiana Jones and the Last Crusade, and National Treasure to have the best chance of finding treasure in my treasure hunts or chases.

Riley's Treasure Chase pirate flag (photo by author)

THE PIRATE

Riley's father Michael thinks like a crafty pirate or clever privateer. Pirates are not bound by property rules, so they can be extra sneaky when hiding their treasure. So Michael is the pirate in this tale. You need to think like a crafty pirate to beat the pirate at his own game. Pirates want to keep their treasure hidden forever, so they will do their best to deceive anyone who tries to capture their prize.

Until one of you finds the hidden treasure, the Pirate's game goes on. If you get close and don't find the treasure, the crafty pirate may fall over laughing while drinking his favorite Pirate's Root Beer.

The prize will be different, and the place this treasure is hidden will be different, too, from *Lady Liberty's Treasure Hunt*. This will keep anyone from comparing the two books for hints or clues. Pirates are too crafty and sneaky to fall for that move.

Riley liked the treasure-hiding idea a lot because he loves children. Pack 79 Cub Scouts and Troop 79 Andover Scouts would go crazy whenever they saw Riley at their meetings because he is so darn cute. Children just love dogs and animals. That is really awesome.

One day, I got home from work, and I was kind of tired but Riley was not having that. He ran and brought a tennis ball for me to throw, then one of his toys. Dogs love spending time with their humans.

The next thing I knew, Riley started giving his Daddy kisses and ran to the front door when he saw me grabbing my car keys. Riley is too smart to be shy about going on walks, car rides, or mountain bike rides.

I smiled down at him and said, "Do you want to go treasure hiding with a Pirate?" Riley jumped up onto my legs, excited to go. Riley loves nature and listening to the birds sing. I do, too.

So we packed up all our traveling gear, snacks, water, backpack, put on the bike rack and bike lock, loaded up the treasure chest, and all of Riley's gear for a Massachusetts trip.

Riley and I like camping, hiking, and mountain biking together. I put a big basket on the back of my mountain bike, then placed Riley's blanket in there, and off we went riding. Sometimes Riley gets so excited that he barks to say hi to others as we pass by folks. Children point at Riley and say, "Aw, look at the cute puppy!"

Riley and I had an advantage because we knew exactly where we were going, and had been there many times before. During our fun outings, Riley got a little tired because his father is so thorough in his research and adventurous in his rides and hikes. We spent a lot of time listening to the black-capped chickadees as they flew about the Mayflower bushes. I love the smell of pine, looking upon a line of painted turtles on a log basking in the sun, seeing a big snapping turtle pass by, or a beautiful red and white woodpecker searching for food. I want you to see these types of things too because life is so beautiful.

SMART PLANS ARE THE BEST PLANS

It's safer to plan a week or so or do chunks over several trips. Your parents, grandparents, aunts, or uncles or youth group leaders will know best how to schedule these outings. Massachusetts Patriot's Day week is a great time to enjoy all the American Revolution celebrations, battle reenactments, and parades. Plan it all, and you will love your family trip to Boston and its suburbs. You can see reenactment videos online on YouTube.com, too. Historic Homes and locations are helpful for learning about events that happened 250 years ago.

Longfellow's Wayside Inn Sudbury circa 1716 among the Oldest Inns (photo by author)

Remember to load your backpacks with water, bug spray, sunscreen, a hat, sunglasses, rain slicker, good footwear, and bring snacks and lunch, too. Check the weather before you go out and plan your schedule. Our Troop 79 Scouts often say "be prepared." Find good places to eat along your trails, like Wayside Inn.

All of our children were in Scouting, and I have been actively involved in Scouting for over 25 years. I can hike, mountain bike, fish, camp, or walk great distances. One time, I walked the same distance the Redcoats walked from Concord to Charlestown. That was about 18 miles one way. Keep that in mind as you plan your days. The Redcoats and Minutemen were really tough, so you have to be, too. Please remember to be very polite, discreet, and leave no trace behind in your activities. This is a very important principle to preserve our environment and fun.

No swimming is necessary (courtesy of Wikimedia Commons Public Domain)

Please no swimming or boating as part of my treasure hunts. No winter searching also.

This is a spring, summer, and autumn activity. Please go sledding, skating, snowshoeing or skiing in the winter but no treasure hunting for safety.

Are you ready and prepared for a fun treasure hunt? Please ask your parents to use their social media tools and their PTA contacts to let folks know about my cool treasure hunt books. I would love to visit your schools, church youth groups, Packs, Brownies, Troops, or large audience events and sign books for groups of people who want to set up events with me. My email is in the front of the book. Thanks in advance.

No rowing or boating in my treasure hunts please (Public Domain)

LET'S BEGIN

Remember this treasure hunt is designed to get you out in the fresh air, learn some American history, and have fun with your parents, family, and friends. Having safe fun is the most important factor. Treasure hunting is for those who always want to smile and stay young at heart. If you're grumpy or overly negative, please stay home. My treasure hunts are for happy folks, not complainers.

WARS ARE EXPENSIVE AND SHOULD BE AVOIDED, WHERE POSSIBLE

The British Crown had spent a lot of money during the French and Indian War from 1754 - 1763. They had sent their Regular Army to fight with their Provincial Militia Regiments in the American Colonies. Further, Britain was regularly challenged by France. These powerful European nations regularly harassed each other and their colonial settlements in North America, the West Indies, and India.

The Crown taxed its citizens heavily in Great Britain, and Parliament then passed a series of taxes on the American Colonies which the King authorized. The colonists considered themselves to be English citizens and were extremely angry about these new taxes, and decried "taxation without representation." No Colonists were allowed to be members of the British Parliament. So they could be taxed but had no voice.

The Massachusetts Bay Colony was the epicenter of the complaints and resistance to the Crown's new taxes so King Charles III discussed the matter with Lord Dartmouth. They decided to send British Troops to secure Boston and enforce the King's will.

1768 Engraving by Paul Revere of the Port of Boston (Public Domain)

THE BOSTON MASSACRE

The British tax collectors kept the collected taxes at the Custom House at the corner of State St. and Congress St. Boston outside the Old State House. Unwisely the British only guarded the building with one uniformed soldier. On March 5, 1770 on a cold snowy night. A group of boisterous young men formed around this soldier and were harassing him, name calling, and started throwing snowballs, rocks and clam shells at him. He called for help, and soon there were 9 British soldiers of the 29th Regiment of Foot defending the building. The riotous mob grew to 300 or 400 people opposing the King's soldiers. Someone yelled out fire, and the soldiers then fired on the crowd killing 5 civilians: Crispus Attucks, Samuel Gray, James Caldwell, Samuel Maverick, and Patrick Carr.

Boston Massacre Engraved, Printed & Sold by Paul Revere (Public Domain)

The nine British soldiers were tried for murder by the Massachusetts court. Seven soldiers were found innocent, and two soldiers were found guilty of the lesser charge of manslaughter. The two guilty men were sentenced to iron branding of one of their thumbs. Patriot's Sam Adams and Paul Revere spread word of this incident, and Paul Revere's engraving based upon another man's original artwork was popularly purchased at the time. Modern artist Don Troiani has also painted perhaps the most accurate image of the Boston Massacre.

THE BOSTON HARBOR TEA PARTY

Another important event that showed the King that the citizens of the Massachusetts Bay Colony were going to resist his taxes and British rule was the Boston Tea Party which occurred on Griffin's Wharf (it is now a great Museum at 306 Congress St) on December 16, 1773. The Sons of Liberty set up a political, and mercantile protest against the Tea Act by dressing up as Narragansett tribe Native Americans. The demonstrators led by Sam Adams and Paul Revere boarded the ships and threw the tea into Boston Harbor.

Boston Tea Party Engraving by E. Newberry 1789 (Public Domain)

The tea protests spread across the US colonies so Parliament responded with the Intolerable Acts that ended self-government in Massachusetts. They closed Boston's Harbor and commerce with their British Man of war ships, and their Army.

BRATTLE BETRAYS THE PATRIOTS

The Massachusetts provincial military commanders took their Massachusetts owned cannon from Charlestown that guarded Boston Harbor, and set plans to secure other supplies for their common defense.

Cambridge resident and Militia Major General William Brattle betrayed the patriots, became a loyalist, and wrote a letter to Royal Governor British General Thomas Gage of the Provincial Militia's plans to secure powder, arms, ammunition and means of war. Brattle also wrote General Gage that patriots assembled at the First Provincial Congress (current First Parish Church) in Concord were urging Massachusetts Militia General Brattle to have his Company ready to "meet at one minute's warning equipped with arms, and ammunition."

Riley enjoying the park in Somerville (photograph by Michael O'Connell)

QUARRY HILL

The round 30 foot tall "Powder House" stone structure on Quarry Hill (current location Broadway at College Ave & Liberty Ave Somerville) was a mill built by French Huguenot Jean Mallet in 1703 or 1704. He was a shipwright and became a miller. The Powder House was sold to the Massachusetts Colony in 1747 and it was converted into a "Magazine" storage facility for the Colony's gunpowder.

In the summer of 1774, in the wake of the Boston Tea Party, tensions rose between the Colonists and the British Crown. Several area towns and villages made up the 1st Middlesex Regiment including the Minutemen and Militia companies from: Charlestown (Somerville), Cambridge, Brighton, Medford, Menotomy (Arlington), Watertown, and perhaps other communities. Some of these units began removing their ½ barrels of gunpowder to place them in safer positions away from the nearby British in Boston.

In the early hours of September 1, 1774 British General Gage sent Lt. Colonel George Maddison and approximately 260 British Regulars to the Powder House. They departed from Boston's Long Wharf in row boats; then rowed up the Mystic River, and disembarked at Ten Hills Farm. The British Regulars then marched over Winter Hill onto North Rd. (now Broadway Somerville) to the Powder House Magazine.

The British Officers then set soldiers as pickets around the area while they took 250 half barrels of the provincial militia's gunpowder. The British force returned as they marched to the beat of their fife and drums. They secured the gunpowder in their boats and rowed back to Boston. This British action caused the "Powder Alarm", and 20,000 or more men marched on Cambridge and rioted in the streets for a week forcing Tories and other loyalists like General Brattle to flee to the safety of British occupied Boston. The British may not have realized it; at the time but as the autumn leaves fell from the colorful trees, the season of change was a foot.

Despite the hard New England winter, many communities in Massachusetts in early 1775 burned with a revolutionary spirit. Soon came spring and with it a sense of impending war. Every surrounding community had well-prepared and trained over 14,000 Colonial Militia and Minutemen Companies. The British only had about 3,000 troops available to General Thomas Gage in Boston at that time, and they were about to kick a hornet's nest at Lexington Common, then at the North Bridge in Concord on that sad but glorious day of April 19, 1775.

MR. JOHN ADAMS

We can't forget Mr. John Adams, who was an attorney and politician. He lived with his family at Old House at Peace Hill (current Adams National Park) at 1250 Hancock St., Quincy, Massachusetts. Adams had a Patriot's spirit for certain.

John Adam's Quincy home and birth place (Public Domain)

John Adams was elected to the First Continental Congress in Philadelphia in September 1774. When challenged by an ardent loyalist to the King, Adams said, "Swim or sink, live or die, survive or perish, I am with my country... You may depend on it." John Adams would go on to become our first Vice President serving under President Washington, then he was elected the 2nd President of the United States. His son,

John Quincy Adams, was elected the 6th President of the United States. Quite a family, and Massachusetts is very proud of their achievements.

A GROWING PATRIOTIC FERVOR

Cambridge's Reverend Samuel Cooke was part of Captain Samuel Thatcher's West Cambridge Company. In March of 1775, Reverend Cooke addressed his Minutemen Company: "Be not ye afraid of them, remember the Lord… and fight for your brethren, your sons, your daughters, your wives, and your houses… These instruments of death, taken up only for our necessary defense under alarming threats, we heartily wish and pray may not be prepared for the day of battle… There at present appears no other choice left us, but either tamely to sit down and surrender our lives and properties, our wives and children, our religion and consciences, to the arbitrary will of others, or trusting in God, to stand up in our own defense." Many people in the U.S. Colonies shared this sentiment.

American Revolutionary War Liberty Snake image (Public Domain)

Provincial Militia on the Battle Road by Monica Vachula (PRR) 2003

THE MINUTEMEN AND MILITIA COMPANIES

We now know that at least 86 or more Minutemen or Militia Companies mobilized, marched, sent warning riders, hid military supplies, or fought along the Battle Road against the British from Concord through Lincoln, Lexington, Menotomy (Arlington), Cambridge, Somerville, and Charlestown (Boston) on April 18 - April 19, 1775. Units from the following current Massachusetts communities were actively involved: Acton, Andover, Arlington, Bedford, Beverly, Billerica, Boxborough, Brookline, Cambridge, Carlisle, Charlestown, Chelmsford, Concord, Danvers, Dedham, Dover, Dracut, Everett, Framingham, Groton, Lexington, Lincoln, Littleton, Lynn, Lynnfield, Maynard, Malden, Medford, Melrose, Needham, Newton, North Andover, North Reading, Reading, Roxbury, Salem, Somerville, Sudbury, Stoneham, Stow, Tewksbury, Wayland, Waltham, Wakefield, Watertown, Wilmington, Winchester, Woburn, and perhaps others. Many more communities not on this list fought for General Washington, fought the large-scale Battle of Bunker Hill, Breed's Hill in Charlestown, and helped to completely surround the British troops in Boston.

General Thomas Gage by John Singleton Copley 1788 (courtesy of Wikimedia Commons)

THE ROYAL GOVERNOR RESPONDS

The Royal Governor of Massachusetts, General Thomas Gage, believed that all the American colonies must serve the British Crown and King George III. The King believed the American troubles were caused by British leniency.

King George III circa 1762 (courtesy of Wikimedia Commons)

Furthermore, the King felt that the American colonists were traitors, and rebels who needed to be crushed by force to restore the British Empire. General Gage was sent to Boston to enforce the King's will. General Gage had approximately 3,000 troops under his command in Boston to achieve the goals of His Majesty King George III. These British soldiers came from England, Ireland, Scotland, Wales, and America.

A GREAT DIVIDE

Reverend William Emerson lived at the famous Old Manse in Concord. Reverend Emerson witnessed the Battle at North Bridge. He was the father of the famous poet and writer Ralph Waldo Emerson. On March 13, 1775 Reverend Emerson spoke before the Concord Minutemen and Militia Companies saying: "Behold God himself is with us for our Captain, and his priests with sounding trumpets to cry alarm against you… to their immortal infamy (British Parliament and Ministry) committing Treason against the Constitution of the Colony."

On March 29, 1775, General Gage issued orders to Lord General Hugh Percy, commanding the First Brigade, to assemble his four regiments of about 1,200 men on Boston Common.

General Hugh Earl Percy by Unknown artist (Public Domain)

The large column of Redcoats marched on the Cambridge Road through Roxbury and Brookline Villages to present-day Harvard Street in Alston. The British hoped to take the land route across the Great Bridge built in 1662 over the Charles River (currently the Anderson Memorial Bridge) from Allston (Boston) near Harvard Business School into Cambridge.

This is the same route that General Percy took with his First Brigade Relief Column of 1,200 soldiers and two field pieces to Lexington on April 19, 1775, after he received his orders at 9 AM. General Gage had issued these orders at 4 AM, but there were mistakes causing delays in delivering them to General Percy's headquarters. This delay caused General Percy's relief column to not reach Lexington until 3 PM on April 19, 1775.

The Green Dragon by Monica Vachula Paul Revere's Ride (PRR) 2003

This is why the Sons of Liberty came up with their famous warning code: "One (lantern) if by land (the Great Bridge across the Charles River into Cambridge), and two (lanterns) if by sea (rowboats across the Charles River to Lechmere Point, East Cambridge, then up the Bay Road - now Mass Ave)." Who were the Sons of Liberty, and what were their purposes and goals? How did they operate about Boston and its suburbs?

A Son of Liberty spying by Monica Vachula Paul Revere's Ride (PRR) 2003

The Colonists had pulled up the planks of the wooden Great Bridge on March 29, 1775, so General Percy decided to march up river to the next bridge crossing in Watertown. The location of this current stone bridge, circa 1907, is Galen Street toward Watertown Square. As General Percy's 1,200 troops approached the bridge, they observed an intact bridge with two cannons aimed at them across the bridge on carriages with no one there.   Percy got quite a gift at that moment.

The British felt fortunate because the Watertown Minutemen or Militia had fled and didn't have enough time to take their loaded cannons with them. These two cannons were very likely two of the four brass six-pound Massachusetts Militia cannons that were stolen by the Sons of Liberty from the British Gun House at the Boston Common in September 1774.

Those four brass 700-pound cannon were placed in wagons, and likely covered in manure. Then the stolen four cannon were boated by the Patriots a few miles up the Charles River from Boston to Watertown. The Sons of Liberty pulled off this action without being detected by British sentinels posted on the Boston Common.

The bridge to Watertown Square, and the Concord North Bridge must have been important strategic locations that the provincial militia wished to defend for they both had two cannons placed nearby. After the provincial loss of 2 cannon at Watertown, it seems Concord Minuteman Colonel James Barrett took better precautions for the safekeeping of the cannon he possessed.

General Gage's Concord spies told him the remaining stolen cannons and other military supplies were at Colonel James Barrett's Farm in Concord. Who was Colonel James Barrett, and what is he remembered for?

April 18th, 1775

This official order was given in hand to British Lieutenant Colonel Smith of the 10th Regiment of Foot in Boston on April 18, 1775, from General Gage:

"Having received intelligence, that a quantity of Ammunition, Provision, Artillery, Tents, and small arms, have been collected at Concord, for the avowed purpose of raising and supporting a Rebellion against His Majesty, you will march with your Corps of Grenadiers and Light Infantry, put under your Command, with utmost expedition and Secrecy to Concord to seize and destroy all artillery, ammunition, provisions, tents, small arms, and all military stores whatsoever. But you will take care that soldiers do not plunder the inhabitants or hurt private property."

British Soldiers in Boston by Monica Vachula Paul Revere's Ride (PRR) 2003

The British Regulars, approximately 700 to 850 soldiers, were drawn from 11 Infantry regiments. Major Pitcairn commanded ten elite Light Infantry companies, Lieutenant Colonel Benjamin Bernard commanded 11 Grenadier companies, under the overall command of Lieutenant Colonel Smith. The Grenadier and Light companies were detached from the 4th, 5th, 10th, 23rd, 38th, 43rd, 47th, 52nd, 59th Regiments of Foot, and a battalion of Marines. The Grenadier company of the 18th Regiment of Foot was also involved in the march toward Lexington and Concord. Lt. Colonel Smith sent Major Pitcairn out first with his 300 British Regulars as the lead force of his column.

Lt. Colonel Smith was told by General Gage to seize the North and South Bridges at Concord, capture or destroy any cannons and burn their carriages. The order from General Gage specifically mentioned brass cannons. Four cannon had been stolen from the Boston Common Gun House by the Sons of Liberty. These six-pound brass cannon field pieces were valuable and dangerous in the hands of an enemy. General Gage definitely wanted them found, recovered, or destroyed. These stolen cannons were a great embarrassment to General Gage, and he hoped to fix that situation with action. His troops likely recovered two of these cannons at Watertown, and General Gage hoped Colonel Smith would have further success at Colonel Barrett's Farm in Concord.

I think it would be great if you have the time to study two of these four famous brass cannons by going online. They were later named "The Adams" and "The Hancock." I had the opportunity to see both of these cannons. I stood in awe of these brass cannons from so long ago.

The "Hancock" Cannon (courtesy of National Park Service Public Domain)

THE BRASS CANNON

Where are these brass cannons now? Wouldn't it be cool to see them because their theft may have precipitated British General Gage sending 700 troops out with Colonel Smith to Concord and then 1,200 more with General Percy to Lexington to reinforce Colonel Smith after he reported the problems at Lexington Common?

Why were these two brass cannons named after Sam Adams and John Hancock? What did they do to earn this great honor? Where were these two men on April 18 - April 19, 1775? Since we discussed it already, you now know somewhat about the British goals, but how much do you know about the Colonists that may have lived near where you live so long ago?

Was your community involved in some way during these events?

Where do you live? Do you live close to Metropolitan Boston? Did your community have a Colonial Militia Regiment or Minuteman Company? Does your town still have one? Please go online and learn more about them. Where did they train? Did they march to any places on Riley's Treasure Chase map or Lady Liberty's Treasure Hunt map? If so, a treasure may be waiting for you somewhere close by. If you live far away, that's all right too, but you will need to get your parents or grandparents to take you on a trip to Boston for *Riley's Treasure Chase.*

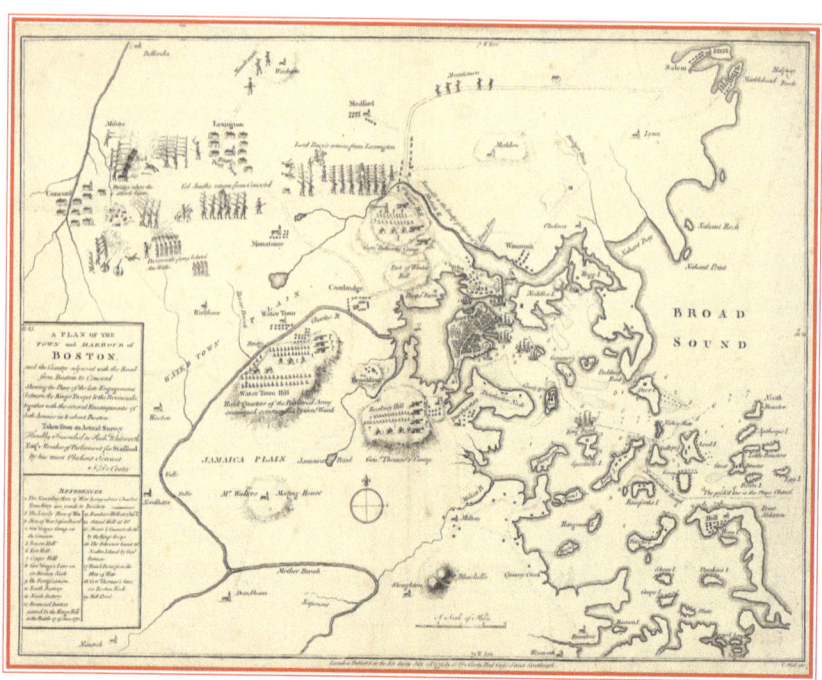

Old Boston Map from author's collection

Spooky Graveyard in Boston by Monica Vachula Paul Revere's Ride (PRR) 2003

NORTH SQUARE

It may be a good idea to ask your history teacher or local librarian to help you learn more about your area's history during the American Revolution. Perhaps you can email your local Militia or Minutemen Company and see if they march or do battle reenactments or living history events? Many of these folks are really smart historians, and they would love to help you learn more. Please tell them about my treasure hunts designed to teach American history. You need to know Minutemen, Militia, Warning Riders or British routes of travel to and from any battle areas in this book.

There may be treasure somewhere along the routes the Minutemen or Militia took, those of the warning riders, or those of the British soldiers. Most of them on both sides fought bravely, and honorably 250 years ago. We respect and honor them. I always pray for all their souls when I am near their final resting places. Cemeteries are full of history, as we teach our Scouts every Memorial Day and Veteran's Day. Freedom is not free; many folks have bravely fought for, and defend our freedom every day. Please honor, remember, and respect our active military personnel, veterans, and police officers.

A brave past by Monica Vachula Paul Revere's Ride (PRR) 2003

PLACE YOURSELF BACK IN TIME

Now you need to place yourself back in time. What happened in Boston, and its suburbs in the decade before 1775? Your parents can help you figure things out or you may ask a local library. Learn to respect and use all these great resources. Please remember to be safe riding your bicycles or crossing the street at all times.

What city did I mention above? That's where you need to start at the oldest house in the city. Somewhere along this long trail in this book is the place where Riley's treasure is hidden. It is very difficult but not impossible to find. The real treasure is in the journey itself and having safe fun with your family. I cannot promise you a treasure chest, but I can promise you great memories of your treasure hunt quest.

Boston 1775 by Monica Vachula Paul Revere's Ride (PRR) 2003

THE OLDEST HOUSE IN BOSTON

From the oldest standing Boston house, go to the nearby famous Christ's Church. Sadly, they would not let Riley in the church, but I went inside alone while my wife watched our dog. Famous people went into that old church, and some of their names are on plaques in some of the pews, right where they used to sit. That's kind of cool; you are now sitting where they sat. What else is neat and important about this church?

Something happened here on April 18, 1775. There is an adjoining spooky cemetery here at night. I heard it may be haunted by a Lobsterman and his black cat. I'm not going in there on Halloween, even with a lantern. Ichabod Crane must have been a lot braver than me.

British Major John Pitcairn leading Troops at Lexington (US Capitol Public Domain)

Major John Pitcairn rests on this church property. Who was Major Pitcairn, and what did he do? Please pay your respects at his tomb, for he fought with honor for his King and country. Sadly, he fell during the Battle of Bunker and Breed's Hill in nearby Charlestown during one of the British Troops brave but foolhardy charges up those hills on June 17, 1775.

Battle of Bunker Hill (and Breed's Hill) by Percy Moran 1909 (Public Domain)

The British proved their resolve on June 17, 1775, by charging three times up those hills to take the field. Still, they lost 19 officers, 62 officers were wounded, 207 soldiers were lost, 766 soldiers were wounded, and total casualties were 1,054. The Colonials lost 135 men, 305 were wounded, 10 were captured, and the total loss was 450. I believe General George Washington or one of his contemporaries later commented that "if the British win any more victories that way, we will win this war."

Now head off toward Cyrus' famous Mount. It's a really important landmark. I know you can find it. When you find a cool landmark, please take a picture there. Sharing great memories is part of my treasure quests.

Next, ask your parents to take you to other cool places in this area. My family loves to eat lunch, dinner, or pastry in the "North Square." That's what it was called in 1775. What is it called now?

Or if you're not hungry yet, please walk across the bridge by the Coast Guard Station toward Charlestown. My youngest son loves the Coast Guard ships. We have been there many times over the years. Byron Preiss even hid one of his *The Secret* book treasures (1982) nearby. Where was one of his treasures found in Boston?

A SHIP THAT IS THE NATION'S TREASURE

There is a famous ship and museum very close by. I love this place and have been there with my children, Scout Pack, and Troop. You definitely need to go there because the sailors on that proud ship had "iron" in their veins fighting for our young nation. Go find it in the daytime. You won't be disappointed.

Rowing across the Charles River by Monica Vachula Paul Revere's Ride (PRR) 2003

After you finish this very cool museum that I have been to so many times, get ready to keep walking. But before you leave this area, look over toward the water for a plaque. Someone very important crossed here on a rowboat on April 18, 1775, under the guns of HMS Somerset during a moonlit night.

Rowing to Charlestown by A. Lassell Ripley (circa 1960 Public Domain)

Now save a little time, and walk across the street to the giant obelisk. Dr. Joseph Warren sadly died here on June 17, 1775. Colonel William Prescott was born in Groton then resided in Pepperell, Massachusetts. It was here on Breed's Hill where he became famous for calmly strolling the earthworks under fire by British cannons, and ordering his men: "Aim low boys. Fire at their waistbands, and wait til you see the white's of their eyes." Colonel Prescott fought in numerous battles and survived the war.

Midnight March Colonel Prescott taking Breed's Hill by J.B. Forrest (Public Domain)

General Warren's Tavern is still open a short distance up the street if you are hungry. My wife Laurel and I love the Warren Tavern. This was one of Paul Revere's favorite taverns. We have been there many times. I try to bring Riley a doggy bag when I can. He especially loves bacon. Who was Dr. Joseph Warren, where was he, and what important things did he do from March to June of 1775?

The British rowed across the Charles River to Cambridge by Monica Vachula (PRR) 2003

THE SONS OF LIBERTY DID THEIR DUTY, AND DANGEROUS WORK

Perhaps your parents should take you along the famous Freedom Trail to see where the Sons of Liberty met at the Green Dragon and who rests in the Granary Cemetery? There are some important figures there. You can learn a lot of history in any old cemetery if you look closely. Don't worry; there are no ghosts in this cemetery. I walked here at night after dinner; with my lovely wife, and saw no ghosts thank heaven.

You have done a lot for the day but should have a flavor for what awaits you next. Don't attempt to do it all in a day. Remember, this quest is a journey of exploration and knowledge.

MYSTIC VILLAGE

Next, ride off toward Cradock Bridge on the Mystic Village (Medford). It used to be a wooden drawbridge. Someone important rode by here on April 18, 1775, near midnight under a full moon. It's time to do some research and figure out where Captain Isaac Hall's home was? Aiden Lassell Ripley painted this location back in the 1960's. Find this place and look closely at the front of this old home; there is a plaque on it. The sign is wrong Revere never made it to Concord.

The Mystic River April 18, 1775 by Monica Vachula Paul Revere's Ride (PRR) 2003

Captain Isaac Hall's home in Medford (Public Domain)

If you are hungry for a good breakfast perhaps drive to 447 High Street. Then head off to cross the Mystic River a second time on the road to Menotomy Village (Arlington). Someone else crossed the Mystic River on horseback twice under a full moon on wet roads after April showers? Who was that?

MENOTOMY VILLAGE

Then on to Jason Russell's "castle" on the Bay Road (current Mass Ave.), and where Reverend John Cutter lived. Who are these guys? What did they do?

Stop and say hi to Uncle Sam, and visit Dallin's place if you find time. Who is Dallin? What is he remembered for?

Next, find Whittemore's marker stone by Mystic St. He was a completely brave, tough, and stubborn hero who amazingly survived the day. Who was Sam Whittemore, and why is he remembered?

Now onto Peirce's Hill; go to Old Concord Rd. (current Appleton St.), where Menotomy Captain Benjamin Locke's home still stands. There is a plaque there by their front door. Someone visited many or all of these places long ago. Have you figured out his name yet? I bet you have.

Good job. Now please get back in the car and drive down Paul Revere Rd. toward Sylvia St. in East Lexington. Guess who grew up there? Someone not all that important in history; you guessed right, I grew up there with my five siblings. We used to watch Revere and Dawes recreated rides on the Old Bay Rd (now Mass Ave) on April 19th as children. It was so exciting.

William Dawes' famous ride by Monica Vachula Paul Revere's Ride (PRR) 2003

ON THE ROAD TOWARD LEXINGTON COMMON, MEETING HOUSE AND BELFRY

A large group of men marched by here too, sporting their crimson colors twice in 1775. Who were they? They were a lot happier marching out than they were marching back, that's for certain. The ones who survived the day must have been exhausted, having marched some 40 miles within 24 hours.

EAST LEXINGTON, HOME SWEET HOME

If you need lunch, Wilson Farms at 10 Pleasant St. is on your way. Scott Wilson is a good friend of mine, and I have been shopping at his family farm all my life. Yummy food and snacks for the whole family. Go in and ask for Scott. He is such a great guy! Look at the majestic view from their parking lot up the hill. That's a great sledding hill in the winter months. I used to race my waxed Yankee Clipper sled down that hill faster than any other kid in East Lexington. I went to Sacred Heart Church and Adams Elementary School (current Waldorf School of Lexington) nearby.

Adams Elementary School before it became Waldorf School (Public Domain)

There is a special marker in front of the Sacred Heart Church by the Bridal Path. Who is Benjamin Wellington and what happened there?

My 6th-grade teacher, Mr. Bob Farias, was the best! He had a motto on his wall: "Give a man a fish, and feed him for a day. Teach a man to fish, and feed him for a lifetime." I sure do miss Coach Farias, but I think he'd be very proud that one of his Adams School students is helping to teach you US history in a fun way. That was how Mr. Farias taught in a positive, friendly way!

From Adams Elementary School (current Waldorf School of Lexington) you can walk to 837 Mass Ave and see the Bowman Tavern where Lt. Thomas Fessenden, and William Diamond both lived.

Bowman Tavern (photograph by Michael O'Connell)

Next, go to 955 Mass Ave and see the home of Jonathan Harrington Jr. What did these men, and their families do on April 19, 1775?

Jonathan Harrington Jr. House (photograph by Michael O'Connell)

Poor Sgt. William Munroe, someone named his house "the home of the Redcoats."

Now more research, then head off toward Sgt. William Munroe's home. There are a pair of 1700's Scottish steel Murdoch pistols inside their collection.

The so called British Major "Pitcairn pistols" (courtesy of Lexington Historical Society)

Historian John Bell had a discussion with British Reenactor Michael Monahan of the British 5th Regiment of Foot. They knew Militia General Israel Putnam was given these steel pistols on April 19, 1775 as a trophy that was captured off a stray horse during the Retreat Battle from Concord through Lincoln, and Lexington.

One of General Putnam's ancestors gave the pistols to the Lexington Historical Society to preserve them for posterity. What a treasure!

Mr. Monahan told Mr. Bell that he believed the crest on two pistols was not actually from Major Pitcairn's family. Historian John Bell then researched them carefully, and determined the family crest on the Scottish Murdoch pistols belonged to the Crosbie Family. He further determined that Captain William Crosbie of the British 38th Regiment of foot fought along all the Battle Road Towns on April 19, 1775 including Concord, Lincoln and Lexington.

A close up view of Crosbie Family Crest on a reproduction pistol (Public Domain)

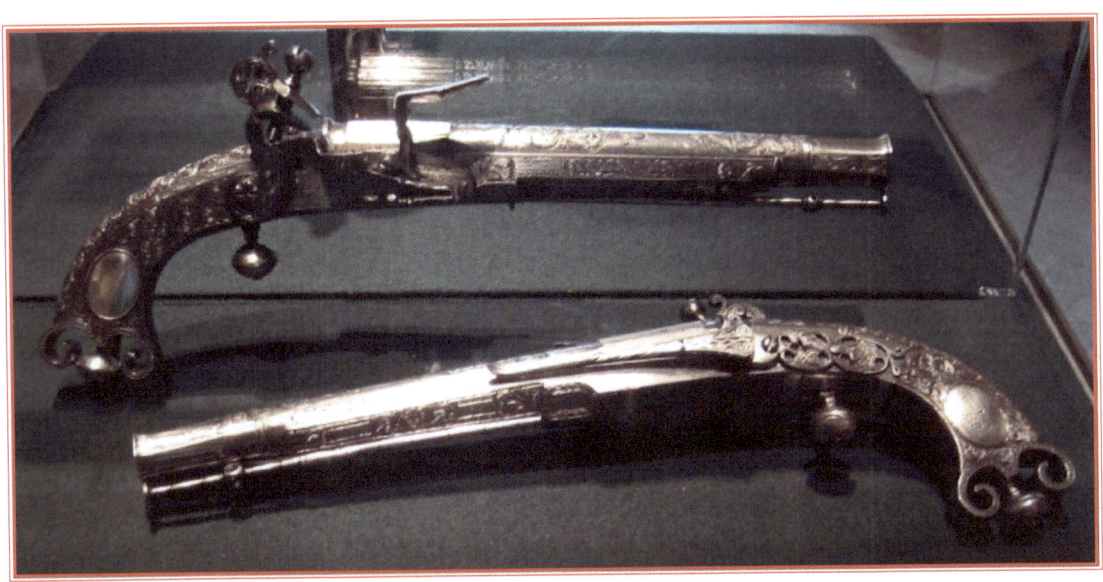

Here is another great pair of Scottish Jacobite steel pistol's circa 1700's (Public Domain)

Who was Sgt. William Munroe, what did he do on April 18 - 19, 1775? What interesting people visited that bright red house?

Paul Revere spreading the alarm by unknown artist circa 1975 (Public Domain)

LEXINGTON VISITOR'S CENTER

From there, you want to go west to the Lexington Visitors Center at 1875 Mass Ave at Meriam St. Go in and learn about Lexington's great history on April 19, 1775. Visitors Centers are always helpful on a journey back in time. Lexington has a beautiful Visitors Center, and you can visit nearby historic Buckman Tavern and the Hancock-Clarke House. What happened at these places in 1775? Lexington has tour guides on their Common in the day time work hours.

Please ask the staff about all the cool stuff you need to check out. Make sure to look at all the art prints about USS Lexington in the Lexington Visitor's Center. I donated them to the citizens of the Town of Lexington many years ago to help teach history about the ships named after Lexington. They forgot to put my name on the plaque, but that's OK.

LIBRARIES ARE A GREAT PLACE TO LEARN

I would then go across the street to the Cary Memorial Library if it's open. Go into the room on your left, and you will see a series of paintings about events that occurred here in town or nearby. Amos Doolittle's works are very important. Lexington's own Aiden Lassell Ripley's Paul Revere prints are also significant to learn about.

You already passed one of Aiden Lassell Ripley's artworks in the Lexington Center Post Office on Mass Ave by Grant St. Walk in to see the friendly postal folks, and look up.

Paul Revere's Ride by A. Lassell Ripley (US National Archives)

Lexington has good places to eat, like Mario's Italian Restaurant and ice cream on the corner by the traffic light. CVS has water to help you stay hydrated, and please check out the historic displays in their front windows.

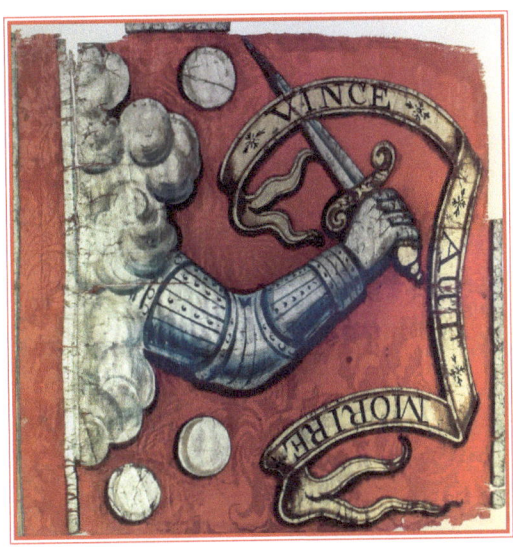

The original Bedford Flag circa early 1700's (Bedford Library Public Domain)

IMPORTANT AREA LIBRARIES

While I'm mentioning libraries, the Bedford Public Library has the Bedford Flag there, and "The Patriot" Sculpture at Veteran's Park is really nice!

The Patriot Sculpture at Veteran's Park Bedford (photograph by Michael O'Connell)

Minuteman Nathaniel Page Grave at Old Burying Ground Bedford (by author)

Capt. Jonathan Wilson Old Burying Ground died in Lincoln April 19, 1775

The Bedford Library staff can teach you about Captain Jonathan Wilson, Nathaniel Page, The Bedford Flag and Bedford's line of march from Fitch Tavern to Concord (6 miles) and their pursuit of the Redcoats back through the Battle Road Trails to Lincoln, Lexington, Menotomy, and beyond.

Bedford's Fitch Tavern (photograph by Michael O'Connell)

Bedford Minutemen form up every Patriot's Day at Fitch Tavern to march to Concord

Upon receiving the alarm on April 19, 1775 the 25 Bedford Minutemen assembled at the Fitch Tavern. As they ate breakfast, Captain Wilson addressed them. He said "It's a cold breakfast boys, but we'll give the British a hot dinner. We'll have every dog of them before night."

Bedford was really important because many towns went that way on their lines of march on April 19, 1775. Bedford has distinct marker signs showing their Minutemen and Militia's line of march.

Bedford's proud of line of march that others soon followed (photograph by author)

Many Minutemen and Militia Companies from several different towns went this way to start fighting the British in Concord along the current Battle Road starting at Meriam's Corner.

The Town of Acton has two important relics behind glass that famous Concord sculptor Daniel Chester French used to make his famous Minuteman Statue.

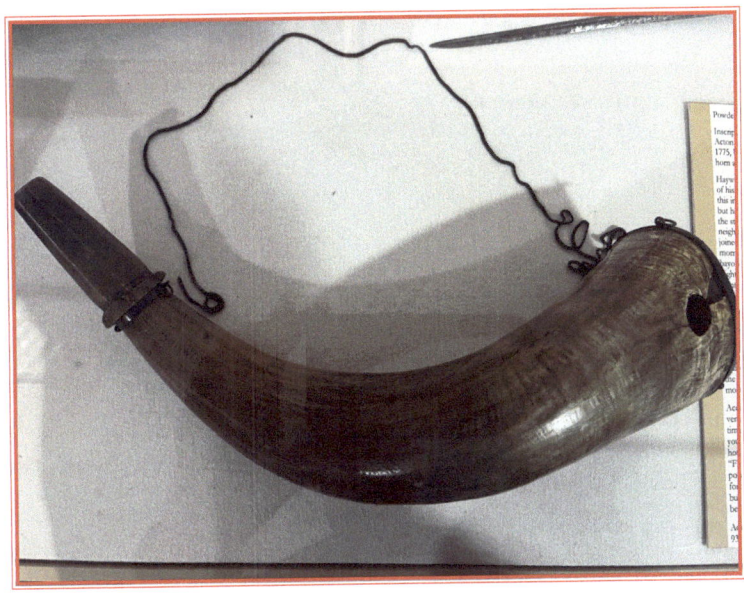

Acton Minuteman John Hayward's Powder Horn (Acton Public Library photo by author)

Please ask the Acton Library staff about Captain Isaac Davis and his company. His magnificent monument is there in Acton Center Square. Who is now buried there with him? There is a minor mistake on the plaque about Hayward; he was shot during the Retreat Battle in Lexington through his powder horn by the Fiske Hill Farm well and the apple orchards, not in Concord. It's kind of sad that Hayward stopped there to get a drink of water, and met a Redcoat who had been inside looting the Fiske House. They exchanged fire, and both did not survive the day.

Acton Minutemen Captain Isaac Davis' plow (Acton Town Hall photo by author)

The old proud public signs of Acton's line of march were replaced with granite markers.

Captain Issac Davis leaves his wife & farm April 19, 1775 (Acton Library Public Domain)

Capt. Davis grave stone under historic monument in Acton Center (photo by author)

CAPTAIN ISAAC DAVIS TRAIL

Acton played a really important role on April 19, 1775. They still maintain the Captain Isaac Davis Trail from his old farmhouse 39 Hayward Road, and their line of march with granite markers across Acton down Strawberry Hill Rd. to the Old North Bridge in Concord. This route is important because the communities abutting Acton and beyond it all went this way on their line of march.

Please learn all you can about this line of march and Captain Isaac Davis. His farmhouse is still there, and he fell first at Concord. I really admire his bravery and sacrifice for our freedom. Captain Davis was a blacksmith, and he wisely made all his men bayonets. After they arrived in Concord, Davis was later asked to lead his men first with their bayonets because the British had them too and used them at Lexington Common that morning. When asked, Davis proudly stated, "I have not a man that fears to go." This Isaac Davis Trail has granite markers to help show you their line of march. Over the bridge, and through the wood many a man would go but not all of them would return home. All granite historical markers are really important to preserving history. Nice job preserving history Acton and Concord!

Captain Isaac Davis Trail Acton to North Bridge Concord (photograph by author)

CONCORD AND CARLISLE PREPARE

Reuben Brown, a saddler in Concord, was sent on horseback in the early morning hours by Colonel Barrett to Lexington to gather information, and report back about the British Troops force and movements. He witnessed the Battle of Lexington, then immediately rode back to Concord and reported what he saw. Colonel Barrett then sent Reuben Brown and Deacon William Parkman to notify surrounding Villages and Towns. He instructed Brown to ride all the way to Hopkinton (35 miles southwest of Concord), notifying every community along the way.

For an unknown reason Brown and Parkman rode together north to notify the Carlisle Village first. At the time, Carlisle was part of Concord and Billerica. The alarm was delivered to Carlisle Lt. James Russell Jr. He instructed Timothy Russell to use his drum to rally the Troops, and for James Kent to blow his horn. The Meeting House bell was also rung to awaken the Village.

With Lt. James Russell Jr. (in Command), Lt. John Heald, Sergeant James Nickles, Sgt. David Hartwell, Timothy Wilkins (Drummer), William Kemp (Bugler), John Nickles, Joseph Nickles, John Nickles, Jr, Ebenezer Hardy, Nathan Munroe, Aron Munroe, Jonas Munroe, Josiah Heald, Jonas Robbins, Nathaniel Parker, Asa Spaulding Jr., and Simeon Barrett.

The Carlisle Minutemen or Militia (17 strong) marched from the Carlisle Common by the Original Meeting House and marched down Lowell St. to Hildreth's Corner Lowell St at Barrett's Mill Rd Concord. This was the planned spot to meet the larger force of Acton's Isaac Davis coming from Strawberry Hill Rd. onto Barrett's Mill Rd. The Carlisle men joined with the Acton Minutemen, and they marched together to the hill above North Bridge.

Lexington's Belfry rang loudly for liberty's sake (photograph by Michael O'Connell)

LEXINGTON COMMON

From Lexington Common, you pass below where the Belfry now sits, and pass the shadow of Lexington Minutemen Captain John Parker's Brown Bess musket heading west toward Lincoln.

Children love Belfry Tower. If you get there before 5 AM on Patriot's Day, they may let you ring the alarm bell. It rang 250 years before on April 19, 1775, on the Lexington Common near the Meeting House. The Meeting House is not there anymore.

Captain John Parker carrying Colonial Brown Bess Musket (photograph by author)

Captain John Parker led 77 brave Lexington Minutemen standing before Major Pitcairn's lead element of 300 Redcoats at sunrise on April 19, 1775 on Lexington Common. Lt. Colonel Smith was directly behind Pitcairn with a column of 400 to 550 more Regulars. Captain Parker is said to have ordered his men: "Stand your ground. Don't fire unless fired upon, but if they mean to have war, let it begin here."

A Reenactment of the Battle of Lexington April 19, 1775 at dawn (photograph by author)

Someone once said, "They were too few to resist but too brave to fly." Captain Parker and his Company were outnumbered 3 to 1 initially, and that number was to quickly grow quickly to 9 to 1 as Smith reached the Lexington Common with the rest of his column. The Lexington Minutemen were in no position to be aggressive or pick a fight. I believe they hoped and thought the British would just march on by and go up the road to Concord since the Minutemen were formed up closer to the Bedford Road side of the triangular Lexington Common.   What those brave few did in life echoes in eternity.

The British Commanders, Colonel Smith and Major Pitcairn, formed their troops on the left and right of the Lexington Meeting House on the common, loaded their weapons, and affixed bayonets. When the Minutemen did not immediately lay down their weapons and disperse after warning, a single shot was heard. Then the British troops fired volleys into the Lexington Minutemen.

Patriot Thomas Fessenden completed a sworn statement on April 23, 1775: "I Thomas Fessenden of lawful age testify & swear that being in a pasture near the Meeting House at said Lexington on Wednesday last (April 19, 1775) at about half an hour before sun rise I saw a number of Regular Troops pass speedily by said Meeting House on their way towards a Company of Militia of said Lexington who were assembled to the number of about 100 (77 confirmed later) in a Company at the distance of eighteen or twenty rods from said Meeting House, and after they passed said Meeting House, I saw three Officers on horseback advance to the front of the Regulars, when one of them being within six rods of militia cried out, Disperse you Rebels immediately, on which he brandished his sword over his head three times, mean while the second Officer who was about 2 rods behind him fired a Pistol pointed at said Militia, and the Regulars kept huzzaing til he had finished brandishing his sword, and when he thus finished brandishing his sword he pointed it down towards said Militia, and immediately on which the said Regulars fired a volley at the Militia, and then I ran off as fast as I could, while they continued firing til I got out of their reach. I further testify that as soon as the Officer cried out, Disperse you rebels, the said Company of Militia dispersed every way as fast as they could, and while they were dispersing the Regulars kept firing on them incessantly, and further saith (say) not."

British artist William Barnes Wollen completed the below work in 1910 for the British National Army Museum London, United Kingdom perhaps depicting the Battle of Lexington Common on April 19, 1775 at dawn from a British perspective.

Battle of Lexington by William Barnes Wollen National Army Museum (Public Domain)

AMOS DOOLITTLE

Colonial Engraver Amos Doolittle's depiction of what occurred on the Lexington Common at 5 AM was created a month after the incident occurred by talking with people who observed what happened. His work showed the Colonists trying to retreat as the aggressors advanced and fired upon them. Doolittle's work was the Colonist's perspective on the incident at Lexington.

Lexington Common by Amos Doolittle (Public Domain)

Though there is no proof, it appears to me that the British fired first. I'm a Lexington native; so I may be biased, even if I'm trying not to be. Though I'm of Irish descent; so if any of my ancestors were here, they were fighting with the Irish under the King's flag. In 1775, Ireland was completely under British rule.

British 7th Regiment of Foot Flag captured October, 1775 (West Point NY Exhibit)

Try to check out the Dawn of Liberty mural in Cary Hall at 1600 Mass. Avenue. Unfortunately, 8 men died, and 10 more were wounded on Lexington Common during that sad but glorious beginning of the American Revolution. Lexington Reenactments occur every Patriot's Day weekend. They are well worth your time. Lexington has tour guides who accurately teach their proud history. These guides know the area well, and enjoy answering thoughtful questions.

Lexington Minutemen Captain John Parker's grave (photograph by author)

YE OLDE CEMETERY

Now find Ye Old Cemetery at 1965 Mass Ave. (behind the Tremblay's House). Please be respectful when visiting the cemetery, but do visit Captain John Parker's grave. There's also a British soldier buried there who died on April 22, 1775, in the Lexington Meeting House from wounds received during the Retreat Battle near the Common.

Unknown brave British soldier who fought for his nation (photo by Michael O'Connell)

Please take a moment to pray for all their souls. Soldiers on both sides fought with valor and honor so long ago. Interestingly, Paul Revere cut through this cemetery on the morning of April 19th while trying to avoid the British Troops to reach the Hancock Clarke House at 36 Hancock Street to assist Sam Adams and John Hancock. Please visit the Buckman Tavern, and Hancock-Clarke house.

HEAD UP CONCORD HILL

Next, drive up Concord Hill, turn right on Wood Street, then take a quick left on Old Mass Ave. You'll pass Fiske Hill Farm on your left, where Hayward fell. There is a marker there and a parking lot across the street. Riley and I like to park there and then mountain bike ride the trail toward Concord Center. It's a spectacular ride, but be sure to ride your bike under control as the trails are sandy and uneven. Please walk your bike across any wooden boardwalks.

After that, drive or ride west to Minuteman National Park. Be sure to visit the Visitor's Center on the Lexington-Lincoln Line. They run an informative movie every half hour that will help you understand all the events of 1775. They also have detailed maps.

Minuteman National Park Battle Road (photograph by Michael O'Connell)

MINUTEMAN NATIONAL PARK

I often ride my mountain bike in this park. It's really pretty, peaceful, and historic. This historic trail begins at Fiske Hill Old Mass Ave at Wood St. Lexington and ends at Meriam's Corner Corner. If you have two adults, you could drop off the children with one adult. The other adult can drive up to Meriam's Corner, park the car, and then walk or ride east on the trail to meet the rest of the party heading west. One way is over five miles, so having the car at Meriam's Corner saves time and effort. Check out all the placards, homes, and historical markers along this route to learn the history.

PAUL REVERE CAPTURE SITE

In Lincoln on Rt 2A west along the Minuteman National Park Battle Road Trail there is the Capture of Paul Revere site. It has a placard on it which describes the events that happened there, and it has an image of a 1960's Aiden Lassell Ripley art work depicting the capture of Paul Revere.

Paul Revere Capture by A. Lassell Ripley (National Park Service Public Display)

William Dawes got away & rode off toward Lincoln by Monica Vachula (PRR) 2003

Modern Artist Cortney Skinner has done a series of Paul Revere art prints for the Paul Revere House Association. They plan to release a book with his works in 2025. He is a great artist like Don Troiani, and their works are historically accurate. I proudly own a great number of Don Troiani art prints, and several of Cortney Skinner's prints. The Paul Revere House Association does great work keeping our Boston, and Massachusetts history alive for future generations.

Mrs. Mary Hartwell unknown artist courtesy of National Park Service (Public Domain)

MARY HARTWELL OF LINCOLN WAS TRULY BRAVE

Find the Hartwell Tavern, learn about Mrs. Mary Hartwell, and her husband Lincoln Minuteman Sergeant Samuel Hartwell. Dr. Samuel Prescott had rode to her home and alerted her of the British Officers nearby on the road toward Concord trying to prevent the alarm from reaching and alerting Concord. Mary Hartwell then bravely ran to the nearby Lincoln Minutemen Captain Smith's home to spread the alarm.

Mary Hartwell from a window in the front of her home watched the 700 man British Column led by their Commanding Officers on Horseback wearing beautiful Crimson Red Uniforms with fife and drum playing marching on toward Concord in the morning sunlight of April 19, 1775. Mary Hartwell may have thought it was the most magnificent sight she ever saw, if it were not for their purpose. The British Troops formation would have looked like a massive parade in a very rural quiet farm area. Mary Hartwell fled the area to take her children to greater safety away from the Battle Road so she did not witness the fighting on the British Retreat by her home in the afternoon.

THERE WERE MANY ALARM RIDERS

Paul Revere, William Dawes, and Dr. Samuel Prescott were not the only alarm riders. There were perhaps 40 other alarm riders. Concord's Dr. Samuel Prescott alarmed Concord, East Acton, Acton Center, and Stow.

Dr. Prescott brings alarm to Concord by Monica Vachula (PRR 2003)

His older brother Abel Prescott Jr. alarmed Sudbury, Framingham, and Natick. Lexington's Nathan Munroe, and Benjamin Tidd notified Bedford. Acton's Edward Bancroft rode the alarm to Groton, Littleton and Pepperell. Abel Benson carried the alarm from Framingham to Needham. There were many other unknown riders that history has long forgotten. They were all brave Patriots.

Concord's Abel Prescott, Jr. alarms Sudbury by Monica Vachula (PRR) 2003

In *Paul Revere's Ride,* Pulitzer Prize award winning Historian Dr. David Hackett Fischer notes "the midnight (alarm) riders went systematically about the task of notifying" communities that the Regulars were out. They went to Minutemen and Militia Captains, Town Leaders, Reverends, family networks and connections.

Church bells rang, and shots were fired throughout communities long before the British reached Menotomy. The whole countryside was awake, and alarmed by 2 AM on April 19, 1775. The British Commanders Smith, and Pitcairn knew this was a problem by the time they reached Menotomy but they kept marching to carry out their orders from General Gage. Colonel Smith notified General Gage of the situation. Gage then determined to send out 1200 more Troops under the Command of General Percy as a Relief Column by foot across the Great Bridge in Cambridge. Gage's orders were issued at 4 AM but blunders delivering them led to a delay of 5 hours before General Hugh Percy departed at 9 AM with his relief column.

LINCOLN MINUTEMAN CAPTAIN WILLIAM SMITH HOUSE

Find the nearby Lincoln Captain William Smith House. He led 100 Lincoln Minutemen and Militia from Lincoln Center to Concord. The Lincoln men arrived there first to join with Concord's Minutemen and Militia companies.

Lincoln's Josiah Nelson alarms Bedford early in the night by Monica Vachula (PRR) 2003

JOSIAH NELSON WAS THE FIRST PERSON WOUNDED ON APRIL 18 OR APRIL 19, 1775

Lincoln resident Josiah Nelson saw a group of men overnight on horseback thinking they were Sons of Liberty but they were British Officers wearing overcoats to cover their uniforms. They were sent ahead by General Gage to prevent alarm riders from warning Concord that the Regulars were marching toward there. Josiah asked for news of the British march and was struck across the head with a British Officer's sword. He ran away, bandaged the head wound, ran about town to spread the alarm, and then rode a horse to Bedford and gave them the warning. Records indicate the Josiah Nelson served in the Provincial Militia from 1775 to 1776, and he was compensated for this service.

Thoreau Farm Concord (photograph by Michael O'Connell)

THOREAU FARM

Since you are so close by in Minuteman National Park, please use your GPS and head to the Thoreau Farm at 341 Virginia Rd. This is where Henry David Thoreau grew up, and it is about a four-mile walk from there to his famous Walden Woods and Pond. Tours of Thoreau Farm are free, and run by knowledgeable volunteers. Ask good questions, and you'll get helpful responses.

Henry David Thoreau 1854 by Samuel Rowse (Public Domain)

Henry David Thoreau was a surveyor and writer. There is a sundial dedicated to him in the front yard. It's pretty neat and appears to point toward where the sun sets each day. Who was Henry David Thoreau and what did he teach?

SCOUTING MAY HELP YOU A GREAT DEAL IN THIS JOURNEY, AND IN LIFE

Are you having fun hiking, biking and learning about history? Perhaps consider joining a local Scouting unit. They teach orienteering, map reading, hiking, camping, positive citizenship and mountain bike riding among many other great life skills. I honestly think it may help you in your quest. I'm going to try to create patches that Scouts can earn by going treasure hunting.

Three of our amazing Troop 79 Eagle Scouts (photograph by Michael O'Connell)

If you live close enough and wish to visit or join, our Boys Troop 79 Andover meets Thursday evenings currently at 7 PM at Saint Robert's Parish, 198 Haggetts Pond Rd., Andover, Massachusetts. You are allowed to belong to two Troops; if you like doing fun outings, and advancing in your Scouting journey.

Our Troop refers any interested young ladies to our sister Troop 73G at South Church Andover. They also meet Thursdays at 7 PM during the school year. Andover also has a Girl Scout unit at Camp Maude Eaton, 141 Abbot St. My wife and daughter were both Girl Scouts, and we sold or ate a lot of yummy Girl Scout cookies over the years.

I am pleased to support all Scouting programs. Invite me to visit your Scouting Unit, and I can sign all your treasure hunt books. Please go online to YouTube.com and search for "Troop 79 Andover" to see our great video made by our former Senior Patrol Leader and Eagle Scout Matthew Webber. My son Corey earned his Eagle badge, too. What a great achievement! In the front of this book you will find my website, and emails. If you want to learn more about Scouting please ask your parents to email me. You can also check out our Troop website: andover79.mytroop.us .

KEEP ROLLING

From Thoreau's Farm on Virginia Road, keep going west on Lexington Road to the area of the historic Wright Tavern.

Wright Tavern Concord (photographs by Michael O'Connell)

Then head toward a truly sad mother holding her beloved son. Across from them, is the old cemetery depicted in Amos Doolittle's famous engravings. British Colonel Smith, and Major Pitcairn were there on top of the hill. What were they doing in the Old Burying Ground Cemetery?

A View of the Town of Concord April 19, 1775 7 AM by Amos Doolittle (Public Domain)

SOUTH BRIDGE

British Captain Mundy Pole was ordered by Colonel Smith to seize the South Bridge (496 Main St). This was completed by 8 AM. Pole ordered his troops to search area homes. Sudbury soldier Josiah Haynes tried to do reconnaissance of the Concord Center area but the British troops would not let him cross the bridge. He then rode back to Sudbury and advised their commanders that the British had secured the South Bridge with a large force (about 150 Regulars).

Lee's Hill 1775 unobstructed view for miles in all directions (photograph by author)

Captain Pole went up to the extreme high ground of Lee's Hill (current Nawshawtuc Road Concord) and observed a large force of Provincials consisting of at least five Foot Companies and a Horse Troop heading toward the North Bridge. Pole then notified Capt. Parsons of this. Even today you can see across South Meadow Field toward Old Road to 9 Acre Corner, which leads back to Sudbury Center from Sudbury Rd to Concord Rd. These troops were from Sudbury and under the command of Lieutenant Colonel Howe. The horse riders were Captain Loker's Sudbury Horse Company from the Cochituate Village of current Wayland. They were heading toward Colonel Barrett's Farm at 448 Barrett's Mill Rd., and then on to the North Bridge.

GENERAL HENRY KNOX TRAVELED THROUGH WORCESTER, FRAMINGHAM, SUDBURY, WAYLAND, WESTON, WALTHAM, WATERTOWN, CAMBRIDGE, SOUTH BOSTON TO DORCHESTER HEIGHTS

Interestingly, Henry Knox and his noble train came through East Sudbury (current Wayland) from Framingham on the Old Connecticut Path over the current Stone Bridge. In 1776, this bridge over the Sudbury River was made of wood; and could not take the weight of the heaviest cannon, just the smaller lighter cannon.

Knox wisely divided them up in Framingham; and likely sent the heavy cannons up Landham Rd. Sudbury then east on Boston Post Rd. through Wayland, Weston Center, (current Route 20 East) through Waltham, Watertown to Harvard Square Cambridge following behind the rest of the artillery train. There is a Knox Trail plaque at the Stone Bridge in Wayland, and another in Weston Center.

General Henry Knox marker Boston Post Rd. Weston Center (photograph by author)

For unknown reasons, Sudbury got left out on the Knox plaques but it is clear that Henry Knox must have sent some of his heavier cannon and their wagon or sled teams up different roads like Landham Rd. Sudbury to (current Route 20 East) Boston Post Road. Perhaps Sudbury's role in this was forgotten by time but we may correct the record here somewhat.

Sudbury Minuteman Statue Sudbury Centre near First Parish (photograph by author)

SUDBURY MINUTEMEN AND MILITIA

The Sudbury Minuteman and Militia West Side Companies had traveled from the First Parish Church, Sudbury Common on Concord Road to Pantry Rd., Dakin Rd., Old Picard Rd., Old Marlboro Rd., Old Bridge Rd., across Derby Bridge, Commonwealth Ave, Barrett's Mill Road, then across Lowell St on to the North Bridge Concord. They then pursued the British Column to Meriam's Corner with other Minutemen and Militia Companies that were by the North Bridge. They do this patriotic march to Concord each Patriot's Day.

The Sudbury Minutemen and their Fife & Drum Corps (courtesy of Sudbury Company)

EGG ROCK

At the base of historic Nawshawtuc Hill is Squaw Trail. It has a trail to Egg Rock where the confluence of the cold waters of the Assabet and Sudbury Rivers form the Concord River. The original Native Americans, the Nipmuc, lived here on the land among the grassy river.

OLD TRAIN MEMORIES, AND CURRENT RAIL TRAILS FOR RECREATION

I just love trains and the routes they used to take. I have a bunch of cool old railroad lanterns in my study. The old abandoned Reformatory Train line ran through the woods pretty close to the Egg Rock area in Concord.

The trains used to run from their junction and roundabout where the current Massachusetts State Police Barracks is on Route 2 through here, then over a bridge (now gone) over the Sudbury River, then across Lowell St. near the Concord Lumber yard, then across Monument St. through the beautiful Great Meadow, across busy Route 62, through the Bedford Water Treatment area to Railroad Ave. area.

Boston and Maine Train Depot (courtesy of B&M Train Museum Bedford)

There is an Old Boston and Maine Train Museum here in Bedford, and there is a close by old Narrow Gauge Rail Trail that runs by Veteran's Park all the way to Concord Rd. Billerica line. You can also get onto the Minuteman Bike Trail that runs through Lexington Center, East Lexington, Arlington Heights, and Arlington Center to the Cambridge line. These are beautiful recreational trails and my family has enjoyed them over the years. When I was a child, I watched the trains go by on this route in East Lexington, and near my Grandmother's House at 47 Woburn St. Lexington. You couldn't ignore the trains because my Grandmother's home shook each time they passed by.

I should note here that the Bruce Freeman Rail Trail is spectacular, too. I have ridden it from Chelmsford Center to Westford, Carlisle, Acton, West Concord and Sudbury. I like to use a mountain bike for these rides. I have walked or hiked all these areas before with my beautiful wife Laurel, Riley dog, or children. I enjoy the Nashua River Rail trail also from Ayer & Groton, Massachusetts to Hollis, and Nashua, New Hampshire.

WHERE THERE IS SMOKE, THERE IS FIRE NEAR CONCORD CENTER

British Captain Laurie at the North Bridge with less than 96 British soldiers already had his hands full facing off against over 400 Colonials on the hill before him. Once Sudbury got there, the situation would become even worse. Then smoke was observed rising from Concord as the King's Troops burned any military provisions or cannon carriages they found. This angered the Colonial troops, who thought the British were setting fire to the town buildings to burn the town.

IRON CANNONS LOCATED AND DESTROYED NEAR SOUTH BRIDGE MAIN ST. CONCORD

Captain Pole's command found and destroyed three 24-pound iron cannons, burnt their gun carriages, and other supplies. At 9:30 AM, the firing started at the North Bridge, and Captain Pole immediately left the South Bridge going north into Concord Center back to Colonel Smith as reinforcements. Smith had greatly weakened his force by dividing it into four separate commands with different mission targets in Concord.

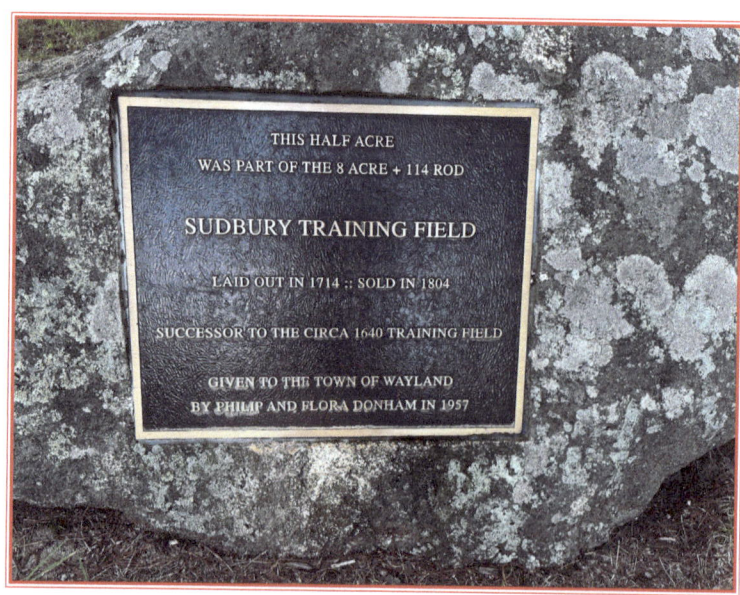

East Sudbury Training Field Glezen Lane Wayland (photograph by Michael O'Connell)

EAST SUDBURY, WAYLAND AND FRAMINGHAM MINUTEMEN AND MILITIA

After 9:30 AM, the East Sudbury (now Wayland) Companies from the Glezen Lane Training Field area in current Wayland; and Framingham Minutemen then crossed the British vacated South Bridge, and went east to avoid all the British troops massed in Concord Center. These East Sudbury (current Wayland) and Framingham Minutemen worked well together to form a cohesive unit. This is really important in a battle, where your life may depend on the other men beside you. Hence the well used term: "brothers in arms."

Two brothers were leaders in each Town's Company so their men worked hand in hand supporting the other. Lieutenant Colonel Thomas Nelson was second in command of the East Sudbury Minutemen and Militia Companies, and his brother John commanded the Framingham Minutemen and Militia.

Framingham Minuteman Buckminster Square (Public Domain)

GAGE'S CONCORD SPIES IN CONCORD

General Gage had sent two spies to Concord, Ensign Henry De Berniere and Captain Brown. They met with a well-known Tory, Daniel Bliss, who was completely loyal to his King. He gave General Gage's vast intelligence on who was doing what and where cannons and military supplies were hidden. Their information obviously helped Captain Pole.

You will see a famous inn at Concord Center, and there is a British gravestone across the street on the sidewalk. My wife Laurel, and I ate dinner here several times over the years. It's a nice place to relax after a busy day.

MANY NARROW, BUMPY WAGON ROADS, AND TRAILS LEAD TO AND FROM RURAL CONCORD IN 1775

You need to head up that street toward a rude bridge. Emerson can show you the way from his Old Manse. Reverend William Emerson lived here on April 19, 1775. Take some time to learn about him, his son and the Old Manse.

The Old Manse where the Emerson family lived (courtesy of the Trustees)

Who is Ralph Waldo Emerson? Who was Reverend William Emerson? What is so special about these men and the Old Manse? Ralph Waldo Emerson spoke these words about the North Bridge fight on the Centennial April 19, 1875, when they dedicated sculptor Daniel Chester French's Concord Minuteman Statue in front of President U.S. Grant: "The thunderbolt falls on an inch of ground but the light of it fills the horizon."

Concord Minuteman honors the farmers who fought here & Capt. Davis (photo by author)

I love Waldo Emerson, so I'm going to share something else he said: "When these acorns that are falling at our feet are oaks overshadowing our children in a remote century… the good, the wise, and the great will have left their names and virtues in the trees." How beautiful was that? You can see the Oak trees Emerson was referring to in Sleepy Hollow Cemetery, where he peacefully rests now on Author's Ridge.

(Courtesy of The Friends of Sleepy Hollow – a natural park and cemetery)

So you have finally reached the Old North Bridge, and it's time to explore the place and learn all that happened here. There are many great books written about this battle by authors like J.L. Bell, and D. Michael Ryan.

Reenactment of The Battle of North Bridge National Park Service (Public Domain)

Cornat Page's Flag carried by the Bedford Minutemen Company (Public Domain)

THE FLAG UNFURLED

At the top of Punkatasset Hill is where the Colonial Militia and Minutemen Companies all massed before they marched on the bridge. This is where the famous Bedford flag first unfurled. The Bedford Flag was believed to have been carried on the Battle Road in Lincoln during the Brook's Tavern, Hardy's Hill, Taner's Brook, and Bloody Angle fights, too. Please do some research: What is so special about the Bedford Flag? Where is it now?

Riley and I walked this hill. There is a stone plaque on the wall across from the National Park Visitors Center on Liberty Street that marks the spot where the Minutemen and Militia assembled. Pretty cool stuff if you enjoy history.

Amos Doolittle's North Bridge – Provincials on left, Regulars on right (Public Domain)

The 96 British Redcoats fired first at the North Bridge; then some of their Mothers later wept as the Minutemen, and militia fired back. Acton in the vanguard with their bayonets paid a heavy price here at the bridge.

Reenactment of Retreat from North Bridge National Park Service (Public Domain)

The British fell back and ran, now outnumbered at least 4 to 1 by the North Bridge. No ninety-six British soldiers could stand against those numbers. The Colonists were mostly armed with American versions of the Brown Bess rifle. Many were well-trained, and had fought previously in the French and Indian War 1754 - 1763 for the King.

THE SHOT HEARD ROUND THE WORLD

In early spring 2024 the National Park Service Archaeologists working to survey the east side (British troops side) of the North Bridge at Concord discovered five varying size musket balls fired by the Minutemen and Militia at the British troops on April 19, 1775 249 years ago. Scientific analysis of the musket balls shows that musket balls were fired from the western side of the North Bridge where the Minutemen were. The musket balls varied in sizes indicating they were Provincial Militia musket balls.

The British Troops used standard size sizes and Provincial Militia used their own weapons of various calibers. The grouping of the musket balls also gave strong evidence that these musket balls were fired by the Minutemen or Militia during the Battle at the North Bridge April 19, 1775. The National Park Service hosted an event at their Visitors Center on Liberty St. Concord Saturday July 13, 2024 to see these musket balls in a small display case.

Bullets fired by Minutemen and Militia at North Bridge April 19, 1775 at 930 AM

I was there, and stood in awe to see evidence of that sad but glorious day so long past. Of course, I then immediately walked into the next room to view the "Hancock" brass 6 pound cannon which may have precipitated General Gage's orders and caused the events that occurred on April 18 and April 19, 1775. You definitely need to see it, too.

Ralph Waldo Emerson described this incident best in his Concord Hymn: "By the rude bridge that arched the flood, Their flag to April's breeze unfurled, Here once the embattled farmers stood, And fired the shot heard round the world…"

Colonel Barrett's Farm House 448 Barrett's Mill Rd (photograph by Michael O'Connell)

BARRETT'S FARM

Colonel James Barrett's Farm was searched, but nothing of value was found. Now Colonel Smith decided to turn back for the safety of Boston. It would be no easy path over 17 miles away with Minutemen and Militia closing in on all sides. Colonel Smith saw Captain Parson's return from Colonel Barrett's Farm on Old Mill Rd. Concord with his 150 troops. At about 11 AM Colonel Smith came down from his high ground observation spot in the Old Burying Ground. At the time, you could see almost every direction in Concord from that high ground observation spot. Now there are buildings and tree growth obstructing the views except down current Main Street toward the historic South Bridge area.

Captain Parsons was not successful in searching Barrett's Farm. Colonel Barrett had already sent his two cannons and military supplies to Groton, Acton, and Stow a couple of days before after getting word from the Sons of Liberty that the British Regulars were likely coming their way relatively soon.

When the cannon arrived in Groton, nine Groton Minutemen or Militia then marched on their own initiative to Barrett's Farm in Concord to help protect the town from the British soldiers. Colonel Barrett reportedly fed them breakfast then they joined with his Concord Minutemen Company. The rest of Groton's Minuteman or Militia Company came later to Concord after receiving the alarm. Groton's many Minutemen, and Militia are buried in the Old Burying Ground on Hollis Street in Groton Center. Massachusetts Militia Major General Oliver Prescott is buried here. He was Colonel William Prescott's brother who fought so well at Breed's Hill.

Prescott brothers Main St by Old Ayer Rd Groton birthplace (photo by author)

Colonel William Prescott's tomb Walton Cemetery Pepperell (photo by author)

Nice job Groton Historical Society, and the Groton VFW (right next door) and for Pepperell maintaining these historic places so well. The small plaques at the base of the weathered stones preserve history for future generations.

Riley's Treasure Chase
by Michael Cloherty O'Connell

Somewhere on this map,
Riley's Treasure Chest is waiting
for you under a full Moon's shadow.
Behave safely, and think like a Pirate
on your adventures with family & friends...

Public-Access Lands, Historic Places & Parks

0 1 2 3 4 5   10   15   17.76mi

Continental Troop Movements

April 18-19 1775

British Troop Advancement

Luther Blanchard's Memorial Stone Old Burial Ground King St (photo by author).

Littleton's Minutemen and Militia honored or buried in their Old Burial Ground include: Calvin Blanchard, Luther Blanchard, Nathan Chase, Enoch Dole, James Dutton, Lt. Daniel Kimball, Nathaniel Proctor, Colonel Jonathan Reed, Peter Reed, Lt. Samuel Reed, Captain John Russell, Moses Sanderson, Lt. Samuel Tuttle, Daniel Whitcomb, Charles White, John Wood and Peter Wright. Littleton also has men buried at the West-lawn Cemetery who fought during the American Revolution: Erza Baker, Matthew Brooks, John Dodge, Rev. Edmund Foster, Nathaniel Johnson, Stephen Pingree, Colonel John Porter, Noah Sterns, and Samuel White.

Old Hosmer Farm – Blanchard stone at 139 Prospect St (Acton Historical Society)

Boxborough's pride of their son, Luther Blanchard (Public Display)

Luther Blanchard and his brother were born in the Boxborough Village of Littleton (circa. 1714). Boxborough was later incorporated as a town in 1783. The Blanchard brothers then lived and worked on Hosmer's Farm at 139 Prospect St Acton, and responded from here to join the Captain Davis' march to North Bridge in Concord. Therefor, Boxborough, Littleon, and Acton may all take pride in these brave young men.

THE BRITISH PREPARE TO LEAVE CONCORD CENTER AND START BACK FOR BOSTON

Captain Parsons had safely marched his troops past the Colonials and crossed over the North Bridge, seeing two dead British soldiers there. Concord Captain John Buttrick's men did not fire on them because Colonel James Barrett had ordered them not to fire first.

Concord Colonel James Barrett is buried at Old Hill Burying Ground (photo by author)

Concord Captain John Buttrick is buried near his Colonel (photo by author)

Colonel Smith sent out his Light Companies as skirmishers on his left side (northeast), placed two Light Infantry Companies on his right flank (southeast), and had a rear guard watching west. The Light Infantry kept a wary eye to the northeast at the Militia and Minute Man Companies that were shadowing them, flanking them, or out distancing them toward Meriam's Corner.

At this point, Colonel Smith ordered his troops to head back to Boston the same way they had come. His Grenadiers and Marines began their march toward Lincoln, and Lexington.

The Home of Little Women book – Orchard House Concord (photograph by author)

FROM THE RUDE BRIDGE

From the rude bridge, Concord (Carlisle), Lincoln, Acton, Bedford, Westford, Groton, Stow (Maynard), Boxborough, Littleton, and some Sudbury Minutemen and Militia Companies followed the British toward the Old Manse and then traveled northeast to flank them toward the Great Meadows, farms, fields, woods, toward Author's Ridge and the ridge line that runs from Heywood's Corner beyond The Orchard House (Alcott's) & The Wayside (Hawthorne) National Park Service Historic Homes, Arrowhead Ridge, and to the Meriam House. From 1775 to 1875 these areas were just fields, farms, woods and undeveloped lands with a few homesteads or residents.

Meriam's Corner Old Bedford Rd. at Lexington Rd. Concord (photo by author)

BILLERICA

Billerica Minuteman and Militia Companies had received the alarm at 2 AM from neighboring Bedford on April 19, 1775. They formed up at the Pollard Tavern near Billerica Common and marched down the current Concord Rd. You can follow their green line of march signs from Billerica Common.

Job Lane's Historic House 295 North Rd Bedford circa 1713 (photo by Michael O'Connell)

They then passed Bedford Minuteman Job Lane's , and Bedford Fifer David Lane's homes to Bedford Center near the Fitch Tavern then right on Concord Rd to Old Bedford Rd. to Meriam's Corner Concord.

Billerica Minutemen and Militia line of march to Concord (photograph by author)

Thomas Ditson Jr. was one of these men and he had been tarred and feathered by British soldiers for trying to buy a gun from a British soldier in Boston on March 7, 1775. Young Ditson would have a personal opportunity to even the score at Meriam's Corner and along the battle road all the way back to Boston.

On April 19, 1775 two Billerica men were injured during battle. The Billerica men were great Patriots; they also participated in the Battle of Bunker Hill, Battle of Bennington Vermont & New York line, and the Rhode Island Campaign. Billerica's population was 1500 in 1775, and 321 citizens (28 percent of their male citizens) served in the war against Great Britain in the American Revolution.

Please remember these Billerica men who gave the last measure of devotion for their nation: Jacob Crosby, Abel Danforth, Joseph Davis, Benjamin Easte, Ebeneezer French, Corporal Samuel Hill, Captain Solomon Kidder, Corporal Benjamin Lewis, Asa Pollard, Captain Samuel Rogers, Timothy Toothaker, Christopher Whiting, John Wilson, and Nathaniel Wyman. May these heroes rest in peace.

From the Fitch Tavern (current 12 Great Rd) area in Bedford Center toward Concord went a line of different towns' troops up Bedford Road to Meriam's Farmhouse Concord, including Tewksbury, Wilmington, Reading (North Reading & Wakefield), Billerica, and Chelmsford. These men had been told about the massacre of eight Colonists at Lexington Common by 700 British troops and the engagement at North Bridge. They viewed the British as aggressors and knew the day's business before them was grim and dangerous. They weren't afraid but perhaps very ready to fight back.

Col. Joshua Harnden 1770 Tavern 430 Salem St. (courtesy of Wilmington Town Museum)

WILMINGTON MINUTEMEN AND MILITIA

The Wilmington Minutemen and Militia were part of the 2nd Middlesex County Regiment, and had their Training Field by Federal Hill near their Sergeant William Blanchard's home. This location is east of Middlesex Ave., and north of Federal St. near Concord St. Wilmington. Wilmington Center is roughly 15 miles to Concord. Harnden Tavern circa 1770 is now the official home of the Wilmington Minutemen Company.

During the Revolutionary War 260 men from Wilmington fought for Colonial Independence. One great example of this spirit was the "Fighting Parson" Reverend Isaac Morrill who was called a true soldier of the Lord by drawing his sword in the American Revolution. Rev. Issac Morrill's tomb is located beside Wilmington Minutemen Capt. Caldwaller Ford's. The Morrill and Ford families were related by marriage so they are all buried together in the Wildwood Cemetery on Wildwood St.

On March 6th, 1775 after the Charlestown (Somerville) Powder House Alarm, Wilmington voted to call every able man ages 16 to 60 to report with arms, and ammunition for training. Three days later 26 members of the militia formed the Wilmington Minutemen Company under 31 year old Town Clerk and Attorney Cadwaller Ford Jr. who was elected Captain. Lt. John Harden, Sgt's William Harden and William Blanchard were also elected.

Other members of the Wilmington Minutemen Company were: William Butters Jr., Benjamin Harnden, John Winn, Joseph Evans Jr, Jesse Hopkins, Paul Upton, John Eames Jr., Phineas Peabody, Russel Jones, Benjamin Gleason, John Gould, James Tweed, Samuel Eames, John Growling Jr., Moses Pearson, William Fay, Jesse Holt, Joshua Thompson, Jacob Flynn, and water bearers: Nathan Beard, Ephraim Flagg, and Benjamin Taylor.

On April 19, 1775 at approximately 2 AM an unknown alarm rider awoke Wilmington Minutemen Captain Caldwaller Ford at his home at 300 Salem St. This beautiful historic home still stands. Ford had the church bells rung and shots rang out to muster his Wilmington Minutemen and Militia. It is believed that they marched down Chestnut Street to Mill Road toward the current Wood Hill section of Burlington (part of Woburn then). On their march they were told the British were heading toward Concord so they likely went up current Rt. 62 into Bedford Center then followed the same line of march as Bedford, Billerica, Reading (North Reading & Wakefield), and Stoneham Minutemen and Militia Companies to Meriam's Corner Concord.

STONEHAM

Stoneham Minuteman Captain Samuel Sprague (age 56) trained and drilled his three Companies of Minutemen beside the Unitarian Church. Stoneham had 98 men of the Revolutionary War Muster Roll. Stoneham Minutemen Edward Bucknam jr. was wounded by a bullet graze somewhere between Meriam's Corner and Charlestown. Two other Stoneham Minutemen soldiers Timothy Matthews, and James Willay reported they had bullet holes through their Tricorn hats but were uninjured. Captain Sprague is buried in Old Burying Ground Stoneham with 30 other graves of men who fought in the American Revolution. The Sprague family lived by Spot Pond, Stoneham.

Captain Samuel Sprague grave (Public Domain)

The Alarm reaches Trull's home by Merrimack River by Monica Vachula (PRR) 2003

TEWKSBURY

Captain John Trull was awakened by an alarm rider at 2 AM. This unknown alarm rider is in the center of the Tewksbury Town Seal showing their pride at fighting for their new borne nation in 1775.

Town of Tewksbury Town Seal (photograph by Michael O'Connell)

Captain John Trull's grave Tewksbury Cemetery East St (photo by author)

Captain John Trull fired three warning shots to spread the signal. Captain Varnum of the Dracut Minutemen heard this alarm across the Merrimack River. Captain Trull then rode his horse from near the current Trull Golf Course, River Rd. Tewksbury, Trull St. or Fiske St. area to Lowell St., North St., East St. to the current Lady Liberty Sculpture at Tewksbury Cemetery (Captain Trull is buried near here), Lee Street to the Town Common, and there he formed up his men.

They then marched up Chandler St. (Tewksbury has several line of march granite marker stones) past the current Oblate Center then going up Chandler St. Tewksbury marched to Billerica Common, up Concord Rd to Bedford Center, then right on Concord Rd Bedford, left on Old Bedford Rd to Meriam's Corner Concord.

Colonel John Robinson Home before it burnt down in 1937 (courtesy of Freedom's Way)

WESTFORD'S COLONEL JOHN ROBINSON TRAIL

Westford Lt. Colonel John Robinson was awoken with the alarm at his home (current 17 Robinson Rd.) Unfortunately his home burnt down years ago. Robinson ordered his men to march to Concord's North Bridge. Then Lt. Colonel Robinson; and several others mounted horseback, and went ahead to the hill above the North Bridge in Concord to confer with other Minutemen and Militia Officers present. Lt. Colonel Robinson and his party arrived in time to participate in the provincial response to the British Regulars in Concord. He witnessed "the shot heard round the world" at North Bridge Concord.

Colonel John Robinson's grave Westlawn Cemetery Westford (photo by author)

The remainder of the Westford Militia marched 10 miles from Westford Common down Boston Rd, Carlisle Rd, Old Rd, right at West St. Carlisle, right on Lowell St, then left at Barrett's Mill Rd to Liberty St the hill above North Bridge Concord where the Provincial Troops were staging. The Westford Minutemen and Scouts march this route every Patriot's Day rain or shine.

Westford Colonial Minutemen and Militia (courtesy of Westford Minutemen)

The Westford Militia under Lt. Colonel Robinson's command pursued the British Regulars from the North Bridge and flanked them with other Town's Minutemen and Militia Companies to Meriam's Corner. Robinson's men would fight all the way to Cambridge that day. Westford's Colonel John Robinson led his Westford men at the Battle of Bunker, and Breed's Hill in Charlestown in June, 1775.

Chelmsford on the march toward Concord (courtesy of Chelmsford Minutemen Company)

Chelmsford Center Historical Marker Stone (CHC Public domain)

CHELMSFORD MINUTEMEN AND MILITIA

Captain Oliver Barron's and Acting Captain Moses Parker's 105 men strong Chelmsford Minutemen and Militia Companies marched from Chelmsford Common historic stone to Carlisle Center, then down Lowell St to Barrett's Mill Rd to the North Bridge.

Chelmsford's Minutemen are buried in Forefather's Burial Ground (CHC public photo)

The Chelmsford and Carlisle Minutemen do the North Bridge Concord line of march together every Patriot's Day, and Scouts, youth, and their parents often participate. Do some research. Does your Town or City have a Historical Commission or Society? If so, ask them for information about your community. Does your town or city march every year like Acton, Lincoln, Bedford, Sudbury, Carlisle, Chelmsford, and Stow Minutemen? If so, please march with them, and learn about their unit's history.

Do you live near any of the towns that responded on April 19, 1775? Their routes of travel to and from their communities that led each unit to Concord, Lincoln, Lexington, Menotomy (Arlington), Cambridge, Somerville, or Charlestown and all are in play in this fun treasure quest.

Believed to be one of the Old North Church Lanterns (Concord Museum Trustees Display)

ONE OF THE LANTERNS

On your way east you can visit the Concord Museum (53 Cambridge Turnpike) and Ralph Waldo Emerson's home (28 Cambridge Turnpike) on the corner across from the museum. The Concord Museum has one of the two original lanterns that was hung by Sexton Robert Newman, and Vestryman Captain John Pulling Jr. at the Old North Church in Boston April 18, 1775 to signal Militia Colonel Conant in Charlestown of the route the British Troops were taking: "one if by land, two if by sea." That lantern is a great American treasure that you have to see for yourself, if the museum is open! If you live local; please consider joining the Trustees, like my wife and I. Their website is thetrustees.org and covers the Concord Museum, Waldo Emerson's home, and Old Manse among their many treasured locations.

THE MINUTEMEN, MILITIA AND BRITISH LIGHT INFANTRY WERE ON THE RIDGES

Watch out for the ghosts of the British Light Infantry on the ridges monitoring the Minutemen; and Militia flanking the British from the North Bridge by the Old Manse heading across Author's Ridge then behind current author Louisa May Alcott's "Orchard House" (home of *Little Women*), and author Nathaniel Hawthorne's "Wayside" (spooky ghost *House of Seven Gables*) historic homes toward Meriam's Corner.

Many famous authors are buried in Sleepy Hollow Cemetery (circa 1849) at "Author's Ridge." In April of 1775 the "Sleepy Hollow" area and beyond was all rural fields, woods, meadows or farmland. None of the current neighborhoods were there, and rural Concord had a population of 1400 people in 1775.

MERIAM'S FARM

Reverend Ebenezer Foster of the Reading Minutemen Company said: "The British (Light Infantry) marched down the (Arrowhead Ridge) hill with very slow but steady steps, without music or a word being spoken that could be heard. Silence reigned on both sides." The opposing troops were about 100 yards apart when brisk firing broke out. As at Lexington Common, the Colonists said the British fired first, and the British claimed the opposite, that the Minutemen fired first. This is sometimes referred to as the fog of war and sympathetic fire. One person loses their cool and fires; the next thing you know, they are all firing at each other from some distance.

Ensign Jeremy Lister of the British 10th Regiment of Foot said "immediately as we descended the hill (near Arrowhead Ridge) into the Road (Lexington St at Mill Brook narrow bridge) the Rebels began a brisk fire but at so great a distance it was without effect, but as they kept marching nearer when the Grenadiers found them within shot they returned their fire… it then became a general firing upon all quarters…"

Retreat from Concord A. Lassell Ripley depiction of British Troops under steady fire

As the facts present themselves on April 19, 1775, I believe the British fired first at the Lexington Common at 5 AM, and at North Bridge Concord at 930 AM but then the Minutemen and Militia Companies in their anger, and passion fired first at Meriam's Corner at 1230 PM.

Reading Minuteman Capt. Brooks courtesy of National Park Service (Public Domain)

READING (INCLUDING NORTH READING AND WAKEFIELD) MINUTEMEN

Captain James Brooks (later Massachusetts Governor) of the Reading Minutemen Company (which included current towns of North Reading and Wakefield) received the alarm, and was later told what had happened at Lexington Common that morning.

Captain Brooks on their march to Concord through Bedford met Colonel Ebenezer Bridge of Billerica. Bridge reportedly said: " I am glad you have come up. We will stop here and give our men some refreshment and then push on to Concord." Brooks replied "my men have just refreshed themselves and I think there is no time to be lost; with your leave, I will go ahead."

Captain Brooks reached Meriam's Corner (current Old Bedford Rd by Lexington St.) Concord and halted until he saw the British Column of about 700 Redcoats cross over the narrow wooden bridge over the wide Mill Brook. Brooks watched the British Light Infantry flank guard fall in with the main column to cross the narrow bridge.

At approximately 1230 PM Captain Brooks, finding his position could not be outflanked, ordered his men to advance and take a position by Meriam's Farm with good cover from a barn, and stonewalls around it. Brooks then ordered his men to fire on the Redcoats near the bridge. The British fired one volley back then kept retreating toward Lincoln.

British Rear Guard crossed Mill Brook & returned fire with a volley (NPS public image)

Brooks reported later that effects of their fire on the bridge resulted in 9 British casualties in dead or wounded men. The men that sadly died here are buried near the corner under the memorial stone in honor of the British Soldiers. May they rest in peace.

Several British Troops were buried here at Meriam's Corner (photograph by author)

There is a historical marker stone on the corner that states "from Meriam's Corner to Charlestown (16 miles and a 6 ½ hour march) the British Troops were under a hot fire."

THE BATTLE ROAD

The Concord Minutemen, Acton Minutemen, Carlisle Minutemen, Bedford Minutemen, and Lincoln Minutemen all pursued and fired upon the British from their rear and flanks. Stow, Groton, and three companies of Westford Minutemen and Militia harassed the British rearguard with incessant fire as the Column of approximately 700 soldiers continued east on the current Battle Road toward Lincoln.

The Minutemen and Militia Companies were in pursuit of the British Column. The Minutemen and Militia Companies arriving from Bedford Center all ran through the Great Field, meadows, and woods to chase, and fire upon the British up Hardy's Hill toward Brook's Tavern. Lieutenant Colonel Thomas Nixon and his Sudbury (Wayland) Regiment were with his older brother John Nixon's 53-man Framingham Companies. They poured down a crushing fire upon the British Troops. Bedford Captain Jonathan Wilson died here near Taner's Brook as British flankers did their deadly best to protect their column.

Bedford Capt. Jonathan Wilson & two others fell by Frank T. Merrill (Public Domain)

The Colonists have been estimated to be 1200 to 2000 Provincial Militia on the Battle Road between Lincoln and Lexington. We know the British started out from Boston initially with around 700 to 850 men. Colonel Smith was now outnumbered by either 2 or 3 Militia & Minutemen to 1 Regular British Soldier, running low on ammunition, and likely water. General Percy's British Relief Column of 1200 men marched out of Boston much later across Roxbury Neck, then west to Allston then across the Great Bridge through Cambridge toward Menotomy, and Lexington.

Battle of the Blood Angle at Lincoln by Lt. William R. Barker, US Army, WW2 DSC

WOBURN MINUTEMEN AND MILITIA

Major Loammi Baldwin lived at 2 Alfred St in Woburn. There is a statue of Major Baldwin across from the nice Baldwin Bar & Restaurant on Alfred St.   Baldwin received the alarm and formed up his men. Records indicate 200 Woburn Minutemen, and Militia fought that day. He gathered his men at the Woburn Common and they marched west on current Main St. to Russell St through Duranville into Lexington on current East St to Adams St. Baldwin and his Troops heard the great blasts of the British volleys. They arrived at Lexington Common after the British had departed up Concord Hill toward Lincoln. The Woburn men saw the eight dead men on Lexington Common plus the other 10 folks badly wounded by the British gunfire.

At the Dawn of Liberty near Lexington Common Asahel Porter fell (photo by author)

WINCHESTER'S INVOLVEMENT ON APRIL 19, 1775

The Jim Dobbin's tribute to the White Horsemen (of Winchester) in the *Unsung Heroes of the American Revolution* piece of the Boston Traveler (reprinted in the Woburn Journal on July 29, 1887) about Hezekiah Wyman (age 55); setting off from his 195 Cambridge Street (near Wildwood St.) home in Winchester on his White Horse, appears to be a bit of a stretch of the imagination.

According to the Daughters of the American Revolution, a Hezekiah Wyman served in Captain Samuel Belnap's 1st Woburn Company, under Colonel Eleazer Brooks, 2nd Middlesex Regiment. We know that Woburn fought well at the Bloody Angle in Lincoln, and in the Retreat Battle back toward Boston. It seems unlikely that a White Horse was ridden during these events by that Hezekiah Wyman but that does not mean that he did not fight bravely on foot throughout the day. Only Officers, Cavalrymen, Alarm Riders or Messengers rode horses, and few used them on April 19, 1775 to avoid being easy targets by their adversaries.

Records can not verify that the Winchester's White Horsemen's legendary actions actually happened, and the British Troops make no mention in their reports of a White Horsemen harassing them from Lincoln to Charlestown.

Famous historian John Bell found folks named Hezekiah Wyman that served in the Provincial Militia but he has written that this White Horsemen Tale may be a myth. I will defer to his expert judgment here until more evidence is developed that the White Horsemen truly existed, and actually did the amazing things reported about him by Jim Dobbin's in the Boston Traveler long ago.

The facts that we may verify are that Winchester was a Village incorporated into part of the Towns of Woburn, and Medford in 1775. Winchester was very rural with few residents. Over twenty years later in 1798, there were only 35 houses in the current boundaries of Winchester. Therefor, the number of Patriots from Winchester that fought in the American Revolution was very small.

On April 19, 1775 when the alarm reached the Village of Winchester; Lt. Caleb Brooks, and John Symmes joined their Medford Company. Captain Samuel Belknap, and Captain Jonathon Fox joined their Woburn Companies and marched with them toward Lexington.

WOBURN'S REVENGE FOR ASAHEL PORTER'S SENSELESS KILLING

Major Baldwin, and his Woburn Troops observed Asahel Porter's dead body. Porter was an unarmed Woburn Farmer; on his way to sell his goods at Boston, when he was seized by the British Troops in Menotomy. Another Woburn farmer with him was Josiah Richardson. When the British released them near the current Lexington Visitor's Center Mass. Ave at Meriam Street; Richardson walked, but Porter ran in fear so a British Soldier or Officer shot him to death. This shot may have triggered the British sympathetic fire upon Captain Parker's Lexington Minuteman Company near by on the Common. Major Baldwin, and his men were ready to even the score for what had happened at Lexington Common that morning.

Woburn Minutemen Major Laommi Baldwin was a talented leader (Public Monument)

Major Baldwin and his Woburn Minutemen marched up Concord Hill into Lincoln then Concord. Baldwin observed the British and Minutemen exchanging fire in the distance by Meriam's Corner. He decided to walk back up that Battle Road in Lincoln and find good cover positions for his Troops. The Woburn Minutemen and Militia were waiting for the British behind strong cover in concealed positions on both flanks. The Lincoln Minutemen under Colonel Abijah Pierce were here as well. These units and all the others around them laid down a withering fire. Eight Redcoats died here, and about 22 were injured.

At about 1 PM on April 19, 1775 Woburn Minutemen Daniel Thompson, and his two brothers took positions at the Hartwell Farm on the Battle Road in Lincoln awaiting the British Troops. Daniel was an excellent marksman, and reportedly shot several British Soldiers before a Grenadier shot him. Daniel Thompson died at the Hartwell Farm barn, and his brother brought him home to Woburn.

Daniel Thompson's Grave (Woburn Historical Society)

Major Baldwin, Daniel Thompson and Ashahel Porter are buried in Woburn's First Burial ground on Park St. near Centre St. behind the current Baptist Church in Woburn Square. Major Loammi Baldwin was a great hero of the American Revolutionary War. He and his regiment fought in Boston, then New York and New Jersey under General George Washington.

First Burial Ground Woburn (photograph by Michael O'Connell)

From Meriam's Corner Concord, through the Bloody Angle Lincoln, Parker's Revenge, and Fiske Hill, so many British fell wounded or dead, but so did the Minutemen in this vicious fight.

Parker's Revenge at Bluff's near Fiske Hill Lexington unknown artist (Public Domain)

PARKER'S REVENGE

Captain John Parker after taking care of his dead and wounded Lexington Minutemen on their Common had reformed his men; and was determined to march west, following suit sometime after the Woburn Companies. Parker and his perhaps sixty or more men would get their revenge here for what had happened at dawn on the Lexington Common.

Lexington Minuteman Nathan Munroe said: "About the middle of the forenoon (2 PM April 19, 1775) Captain John Parker having collected part of his Company, I being with them, determined to meet the Regulars on their Retreat from Concord. We met the Regulars in the bounds of Lincoln (by the Tabitha Nelson House Lincoln-Lexington line by the current Battle Road Trail off Airport Rd. Lexington). We fired upon them, and continued to so until they met their reinforcement in Lexington (General Percy's 1200 man Relief Column with two field pieces arrived by "O'Connell's Corner" Mass. Ave at Winthrop Rd.)" The running battle between all the Minutemen and Militia Companies against the British troops from Parker's Revenge site (Lincoln/Lexington line) to the Menotomy (current Arlington) line is sometimes called the Second Battle of Lexington.

Parker's Revenge fight by unknown artist (National Park Service Public Display)

Parker had positioned his men on an elevated wooded, rocky hillside right across from a small bridge over a brook that crossed the road in front of Tabitha Nelson's home to where the current Battle Road Trail currently is.

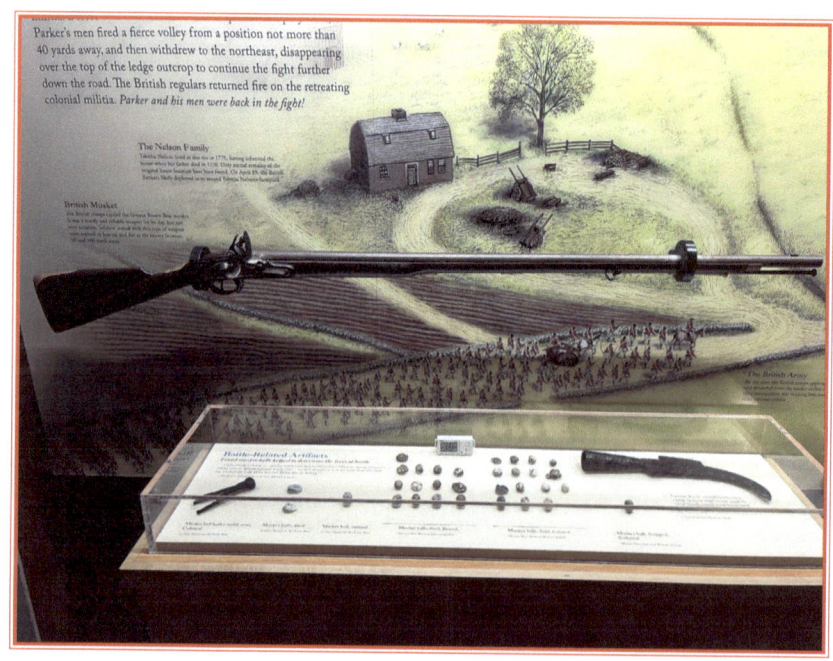

Minuteman National Park on the Battle Road (NPS Parker's Revenge Public Display)

In 2019 the National Park Service team discovered 9 bullets here within about 80 yards of each other showing the close range of the battle here. These bullets are currently housed in a display at the nearby National Park Center Visitors Center on the Lexington & Lincoln Line (a short walk to Parker's Revenge site).

Reenacting British Officers Colonel Smith & Major Pitcairn led the retreat (NPS photo)

British Colonel Smith got injured from their fire upon him and his Troops. The British Light Infantry charged about the hill to fight and pursue the Minutemen. The British Column then continued their march up the dirt road. The Lexington men kept up their fire upon the British from cover, then would retreat back, reload to find new positions to fire from behind trees or walls. All of the Minutemen and Militia Companies were fighting this way. They fought as Companies but also it was one man shooting himself, running away, picking another new good position behind cover, and firing again. They learned these tactics from those who fought for the British in the French and Indian War 1754 - 1763.

Provincial Militia using cover, shoot then run to a new spot, and fire again (NPS photo)

CAMBRIDGE MILITIA

Captain Samuel Thatcher's West Cambridge Militia (77 men) had marched 14 miles out after Colonel Smith's Column. Thatcher's wife Mary Brown was from Lexington, and he and his soldiers saw the sad scene at Lexington Common. They were waiting on Fiske Hill to give battle. Thatcher's militia engaged the British from Fiske Hill, through Lexington, Menotomy, and into Cambridge. Thatcher lost no soldiers during their 14-mile active fighting with the British troops.

Lt. Colonel Smith's Troops desperately retreat by Monica Vachula (PRR) 2003

FISKE HILL AREA IMMORTALIZED ACTON'S JAMES HAYWARD AND WOBURN'S SYLVANUS WOOD

Across the bluff east back to Fiske Hill Lexington, Acton's brave Patriot James Hayward fell to a wound near the Fiske Farm well. He had stopped to get water at Fiske Farm well, and a Redcoat who was looting in the vacated house came upon him. Legend has it that the Redcoat yelled "you're dead" and Hayward replied back "then you're dead, too." They then both fired their Brown Bess muskets, and both would lose their lives from mortal wounds received in this gunfire exchange. I have been to this spot so many times over the years. Hayward is buried on Acton Common. It is unclear where the Redcoat; who fell here, is now buried.

Action's James Hayward was particularly patriotic because he had a clubfoot from an ax accident long before, so he was relieved from having to serve in the Militia. When he saw Captain Isaac Davis marching his Acton Minutemen toward Concord, he joined them with a musket and was ready to fight. That was a really long walk (maybe 14 miles or more) with a bad foot and under fire at North Bridge, Meriam's Corner, through all the fighting on the Battle Road in Lincoln, then to the Fiske Farm (currently on Old Mass Ave by Wood St. Lexington). Near here Woburn resident Sylvanus Wood; who was with the Lexington Minutemen Company at dawn, was incredibly bold and courageous. He chased the Redcoats toward Concord then arrested a British Grenadier who fell out of the march with the column during the retreat.

Riley and I at my beloved Lexington (on my last day as a Police Officer 1983 – 2023).

Riley and I have walked or ridden on a mountain bike on all of these historic trails and routes a great many days. Historic places are really special. We would do well to protect them for future generations. Please pickup any trash you see, and leave no trace behind. Thank you.

1775 Engraving "A View of South Part of Lexington" by Amos Doolittle (Public Domain)

GENERAL PERCY ARRIVES TO SAVE COLONEL SMITH'S COLUMN

The rest of the British had to flee eastward back toward Lexington Common (about a mile away downhill). The British seemed completely lost near Lexington Common, but General Percy arrived with his two 6-pound cannon pieces and fired a shot right through the Lexington Meeting House where the eight dead Colonists had been placed. Percy's cannon fire frightened, and scattered many of the pursuing Minutemen and Militia companies. General Percy also set nearby homes on fire to create a smoke cover for the British soldiers, as shown in above Amos Doolittle's engraving.

General Percy's Royal Artillery 6 pound field pieces were fired to cover their retreat (NPS)

GENERAL PUTNAM AND GENERAL WARREN ARRIVE IN LEXINGTON

Connecticut Major General Israel Putnam, and Massachusetts Militia Major General Joseph Warren took charge of the scattered Minutemen; and Militia Companies on the Bay Road just west of the Munroe Tavern Lexington. They ordered their Troops to flank the British on both sides and fight house to house and barn to barn all the way back to Boston. Major General Warren died in June 1775 at Bunker Hill. He is buried in Forest Hill Cemetery West Roxbury near his alarm rider William Dawes (who rode with Paul Revere April 19, 1775 from Lexington to the Lincoln capture site on the Battle Road in Minuteman National Park).

FROM PERCY'S HEADQUARTERS MUNROE TAVERN TOWARD MENOTOMY

General Percy took command, and rallied all the troops at the Munroe Tavern Lexington. He set up a field hospital, and temporary headquarters. Percy quickly watered, fed and reorganized all of the British Forces. Treating the wounded was the priority so they could then continue back to Boston.

General Percy's Temporary Headquarters at Munroe Tavern (Public Domain)

Then he pressed on east using his cannon as necessary, on the Bay Road heading toward East Lexington, and beyond into Menotomy by the Foot of Rocks.

The Battle at the Foot of Rocks by A. Lassell Ripley (author's collection)

Where is this famous place? I grew up close to Arlington Heights, and I'm sad this important historic place was not better preserved. Former Lexington resident Aiden Lasell Ripley did amazing research and art work in the 1960's about 1775.

Gen. Percy led the retreat with assistance from Major Pitcairn (NPS Public Domain)

With Percy's Column reinforcing Colonel Smith's men on their retreat to Boston, the British Regulars were once again outnumbered by over 2000 militia and Minute Men gathered in Menotomy (Arlington), a crossroads village of West Cambridge.

April 19, 1775 weather was clear and dry, by afternoon there was increasing wind from the west. Smoke from the firing of their own muskets hovered over the retreating column. It became difficult for the Regulars to aim their muskets at snipers hiding in houses and behind trees and stone walls. But militia firing on the rear of the column found that the troops, clad in their Red Coats, were hardly camouflaged by the gun smoke. These conditions forced Percy to order his troops to enter dwellings and clear them of snipers. The flanks sent north and south of the main column through Menotomy (Arlington) were an attempt to regain an advantage through surprise.

British Troops were invading, and searching homes in Menotomy (NPS Public Domain)

By late afternoon, Dr. Joseph Warren headed east from Lexington near Munroe Tavern to join the fighting at Foot of the Rocks in Menotomy. Considered one of the most charismatic of the patriot leaders, Warren was drawn to the fight, believing that to truly lead, one must lead in battle as well. Joseph Warren died two months later at the battle of Breed's Hill and Bunker Hill.

At the end of the day on April 19th the British suffered heavier losses than the colonists. More than half of the fatalities on both sides occurred in Menotomy. Of the 25 colonial fatalities there, only three were Menotomy residents. Citizens returned to claim their fallen loved ones from what was described as "the bloody fields of Menotomy" where horses; and cattle lay dead, and homes with broken windows were perforated with musket ball holes.

The Fight at Jason Russell House by Ruth L. Berry 1975 (Arlington Historical Society)

General Percy would lead his men through a vicious Menotomy Village battle in the current Arlington Center near the Jason Russell House. Within a half-mile of this location; about 40 British fell, and 20 Colonists. The great staff at the Jason Russell House will be pleased to tell you all about what happened here on that important day in history.

NORTH CAMBRIDGE

The British kept going east and crossed the Menotomy River (current Alewife Brook) into North Cambridge. Another group of Colonials was waiting to ambush them here at Watson's Corner (current 2154 Mass Ave).

The Minutemen and Militia targeting the column & were exposed to flankers (NPS)

The British flankers caught them by surprise, killing Brookline Major Isaac Gardiner and two Cambridge men, John Hicks and Moses Richard. British General Percy then wisely cut through Beech St (current Somerville) and up near 145 Elm St., where there was a sharp fight that killed a British soldier here. The British soldier was initially buried here in 1775 but was later interred at the Milk Row Cemetery 439 Somerville Ave Somerville in an unmarked grave. A custom marker now marks this grave: "Here lies a British Soldier who fell on 19 April 1775 serving King and Country." This soldier's sacrifice will be honored by His Majesty's 10 Regiment of Foot or other units representing the King periodically.

Somerville battle location where a British Soldier used to be buried (photo by author)

Over 16,000 well armed Minutemen and Militia Troops surrounded Boston and built a line of entrenchments from Roxbury to Chelsea. The British only had about 2600 to 2700 healthy Troops after the April 19, 1775 Battle Road fight from Concord to Charlestown so General Gage requested reinforcements to raise his Troop strength to 10,000 in Boston. Prospect Hill was secured at the orders of Connecticut General Israel Putnam by building camps and fortifications. Prospect Hill had a commanding view of Boston, the British Fleet at Anchor, and the surrounding countryside. Prospect Hill was called the "Citadel" as a very strong Colonial built fortification in then as part of Charlestown defense.

The Peter Tufts Historic House is on Winter Hill at 75 Sycamore St. It is one of the oldest homes in Somerville. It served in 1775 and 1776 as the Headquarters of General Charles Lee during the siege of Boston.

General Percy used his field pieces here again to create safety for his men to reach Charlestown over Winter Hill and the safety of HMS Somerset's guns.

HMS Somerset 1775 (unknown artist courtesy of US Naval Institute)

The sun set as the British troops laid down exhausted in Charlestown. With all the incidental battle, running, and marching about, they easily walked well over 40 miles in less than 24 hours. The British badly lost the day, and these events ignited the American Revolution.

Washington takes command at Cambridge July 4, 1775 (Public domain)

GENERAL GEORGE WASHINGTON'S HEADQUARTERS

On July 3, 1775 General George Washington arrived at the Cambridge Common on the Bay Road (current Mass. Ave) close to Harvard College. He then drew his sword and took command of the Continental Army.

Washington then made his Headquarters nearby at the current Henry Wadsworth Longfellow House at 105 Brattle Street Cambridge.

Henry Wadsworth Longfellow by Monica Vachula Paul Revere's Ride (2003).

This historic home is well maintained by the National Park Service. Longfellow was a graduate of Bowdoin College, famous poet, and became a Professor at Harvard College. Longfellow's maternal grandfather was American Revolutionary War Massachusetts (Maine section of Massachusetts) Militia Brigadier General Peleg Wadsworth. Longfellow's mother was descended from Pilgrim Richard Warren, a passenger on the *Mayflower*.

Henry Wadsworth Longfellow published *"Paul Revere's Ride"* in January 1861. Longfellow was inspired by; visiting the Old North Church, and climbing to the steeple in April 1860. With the imminent United States Civil War being upon them, Longfellow felt it was important for Americans to remember that ordinary people like Paul Revere fought for freedom, and liberty during the American Revolution.

Paul Revere borrows a horse in Charlestown by Monica Vachula (PRR) 2003

"Paul Revere's Ride" poem by Henry Wadsworth Longfellow:
Listen, my children, and you shall hear
Of the midnight ride of Paul Revere,
On the eighteenth of April, in Seventy-Five:
Hardly a man is now alive
Who remembers that famous day and year.

He said to his friend, "If the British march
By land or sea from the town to-night,
Hang a lantern aloft in the belfry-arch
Of the North-Church-tower, as a signal-light, —
One if by land, and two if by sea;
And I on the opposite shore will be,
Ready to ride and spread the alarm
Through every Middlesex village and farm,
For the country-folk to be up and to arm.

Then he said "Good night!" and with muffled oar
Silently rowed to the Charlestown shore,
Just as the moon rose over the bay,

Where swinging wide at her moorings lay
The Somerset, British man-of-war:
A phantom ship, with each mast and spar
Across the moon, like a prison-bar,
And a huge black hulk, that was magnified
By its own reflection in the tide.

Meanwhile, his friend, through alley and street
Wanders and watches with eager ears,
Till in the silence around him he hears
The muster of men at the barrack door,
The sound of arms, and the tramp of feet,
And the measured tread of the grenadiers
Marching down to their boats on the shore.

Then he climbed to the tower of the church,
Up the wooden stairs, with stealthy tread,
To the belfry-chamber overhead,
And startled the pigeons from their perch
On the somber rafters, that round him made
Masses and moving shapes of shade,—
By the trembling ladder, steep and tall,
To the highest window in the wall,
Where he paused to listen and look down
A moment on the roofs of the town,
And the moonlight flowing over all.

Beneath, in the churchyard, lay the dead,
In their night-encampment on the hill,
Wrapped in silence so deep and still
That he could hear, like a sentinel's tread,

The watchful night-wind, as it went
Creeping along from tent to tent,
And seeming to whisper, "All is well!"
A moment only he feels the spell
Of the place and the hour, and the secret dread
Of the lonely belfry and the dead;

For suddenly all his thoughts are bent
On a shadowy something far away,
Where the river widens to meet the bay,—
A line of black, that bends and floats
On the rising tide, like a bridge of boats.

Meanwhile, impatient to mount and ride,
Booted and spurred, with a heavy stride,
On the opposite shore walked Paul Revere.
Now he patted his horse's side,
Now gazed on the landscape far and near,
Then impetuous stamped the earth,
And turned and tightened his saddle-girth;

But mostly he watched with eager search
The belfry-tower of the old North Church,
As it rose above the graves on the hill,
Lonely and spectral and somber and still.

And lo! as he looks, on the belfry's height,
A glimmer, and then a gleam of light!
He springs to the saddle, the bridle he turns,
But lingers and gazes, till full on his sight
A second lamp in the belfry burns!

A hurry of hoofs in a village-street,
A shape in the moonlight, a bulk in the dark,
And beneath from the pebbles, in passing, a spark
Struck out by a steed that flies fearless and fleet:
That was all! And yet, through the gloom and the light,
The fate of a nation was riding that night;
And the spark struck out by that steed, in his flight,
Kindled the land into flame with its heat.

He has left the village and mounted the steep,
And beneath him, tranquil and broad and deep,
Is the Mystic, meeting the ocean tides;
And under the alders, that skirt its edge,
Now soft on the sand, now loud on the ledge,

Is heard the tramp of his steed as he rides.

It was twelve by the village clock
When he crossed the bridge into Medford town.
He heard the crowing of the cock,
And the barking of the farmer's dog,
And felt the damp of the river-fog,
That rises when the sun goes down.

It was one by the village clock,
When he galloped into Lexington.
He saw the gilded weathercock
Swim in the moonlight as he passed,
And the meeting-house windows, blank and bare,
Gaze at him with a spectral glare,
As if they already stood aghast
At the bloody work they would look upon.

It was two by the village clock,
When he came to the bridge in Concord town.
He heard the bleating of the flock,
And the twitter of birds among the trees,
And felt the breath of the morning breeze

Blowing over the meadows brown.
And one was safe and asleep in his bed
Who at the bridge would be first to fall,
Who that day would be lying dead,
Pierced by a British musket-ball.

You know the rest. In the books you have read,
How the British Regulars fired and fled,—
How the farmers gave them ball for ball,
From behind each fence and farmyard-wall,
Chasing the red-coats down the lane,
Then crossing the fields to emerge again
Under the trees at the turn of the road,
And only pausing to fire and load.

So through the night rode Paul Revere;

And so through the night went his cry of alarm

To every Middlesex village and farm,—

A cry of defiance, and not of fear,

A voice in the darkness, a knock at the door,

And a word that shall echo forevermore!

For, borne on the night-wind of the Past,

Through all our history, to the last,

In the hour of darkness and peril and need,

The people will waken and listen to hear

The hurrying hoof-beats of that steed,

And the midnight message of Paul Revere.

Wouldn't it be interesting to learn from Paul Revere's own words what happened about 250 years ago?

Paul Revere rode into history on April 18, 1775 by Monica Vachula (PRR) 2003

A Letter from Lt. Colonel Paul Revere to the Corresponding Secretary Jeremy Belknap (circa 1798) from Massachusetts Historical Society Collections (slightly edited for spelling and grammar):

"Dear Sir,

Having a little leisure, I wish to fulfill my
        promise, of giving you some facts, and Anecdotes, prior to
        the Battle of Lexington, which I do not remember to have seen
        in any history of the American Revolution.
        In the year 1773 I was employed by the Selectmen of the
        Town of Boston to carry the Account of the Destruction of the
        Tea to New-York; and afterwards, 1774, to Carry their dispatches to
        New-York and Philadelphia for Calling a Congress; and afterwards to
        Congress, several times.
        In the Fall of 1774 & Winter of 1775 I was
        one of upwards of thirty, chiefly mechanics, who formed our selves in to a   Committee for the purpose
of watching the Movements of the British Soldiers,
        and gaining every intelligence of the movements of the Tories. We
        held our meetings at the Green-Dragon Tavern. We were so careful that
        our meetings should be kept Secret; that every time we met, every
        person swore upon the Bible, that they would not discover any of
        our transactions, But to Messrs. <u>Hancock</u>, <u>Adams</u>, Doctors <u>Warren</u>, <u>Church</u>,
        & one or two more.
        About November, when things began to grow serious, a Gentleman who had Connections with the Tory
party, but was a Whig at heart, acquainted me, that our meetings were discovered, & mentioned the identical
words that were spoken among us the Night before.
        We did not then distrust Dr. Church, but supposed it must be
        some one among us. We removed to another place, which we
        thought was more secure: but here we found that all our transactions
        were communicated to Governor Gage. (This came to me through the
        then Secretary Flucker; He told it to the Gentleman mentioned above). It was
        then a common opinion, that there was a Traitor in the provincial
        Congress, & that Gage was possessed of all their Secrets. (Church was a member of that Congress for
Boston.)
        In the Winter, towards the Spring, we frequently took Turns, two and two, to Watch the Soldiers, By
patrolling the Streets all night. The Saturday Night preceding the 19th of April, about 12 o'clock at Night, the
Boats belonging to the Transports were all launched, & carried under the Sterns of the Men of War. (They
had been previously hauled up & repaired). We likewise found that the Grenadiers and light Infantry were
all taken off duty.

From these movements, we expected something serious was to
be transacted. On Tuesday evening, the 18th, it was observed, that a number
of Soldiers were marching towards the bottom of the Common.
About 10 o'clock, Dr. Warren Sent in great haste for me, and begged
that I would immediately Set off for Lexington, where Mess rs. Hancock
& Adams were, and acquaint them of the Movement, and that it was
thought they were the objects. When I got to Dr. Warren's house, I found
he had sent an express by land to Lexington - a Mr. Wm. Dawes.
The Sunday before, by desire of Dr. Warren, I had been to Lexington, to John   Hancock and Sam Adams,
who were at the Rev. Mr. Jonas Clarke's home.

Climbing up the Old North Church April 18, 1775 by Monica Vachula (PRR) 2003

I returned at Night thru Charlestown; there I agreed with a Col. Conant, & some other Gentlemen, that
if the British went out by Water, we would shew two Lanthorns (lanterns) in the North Church Steeple; &
if by Land, one, as a Signal; for we were apprehensive it would be difficult to Cross the Charles River, or get
over Boston Neck.

I left Dr. Warrens, called upon a friend, and desired him to make the Signals. I then went Home, took my
Boots and Surtout, and went to the North part of the Town, where I had kept a Boat; two friends rowed me
across Charles River, a little to the eastward where the Somerset Man of War lay.

One if by land, Two if by sea by Monica Vachula Paul Revere's Ride 2003

It was then a young flood, the Ship was winding, & the moon was Rising. They landed me on the Charlestown side. When I got into Town, I met Col. Conant, & several others;

They said they had seen our signals. I told them what was Acting on, & went to get me a Horse; I got a Horse of Deacon Larkin. While the Horse was preparing, Richard Devens, Esq. who was one of the Committee of Safety, came to me, & told me, that he came down the Road from Lexington, after Sundown, that evening; that He met ten British Officers, all well mounted, & armed, going up the Road.

I set off upon a very good Horse; it was then about 11 o'clock, & very pleasant. After I had passed Charlestown Neck, & got nearly opposite where Mark (Codman) was hung in chains ("Charlestown Common" is currently Washington Street Somerville near the Charlestown line), I saw two men on Horseback, under a Tree.

Paul Revere's Ride memorial marker Washington St Somerville (photograph by author)

(Enslaved Mark Codman had poisoned his master John Codman, and was sentenced to be hung in the gallows in Cambridge then his body was suspended in chains known as a gibbet on a public road at Charlestown Common as an example to discourage others from committing murder).

When I got near them, I discovered they were British officers. One tried to get ahead of Me, & the other to take me. I turned my Horse very quickly, & Galloped towards Charlestown Neck, and then pushed for the Medford Road. The one who chased me, endeavoring to cut me off, got into a Clay pond, near where the new Tavern is now built. I got clear of him, and went through Medford, over the Bridge, & up to Menotomy.

Paul Revere awakens Medford Minutemen Capt by A. Lassell Ripley (author's collection)

In Medford, I awakened the Captain of the Minutemen; & after that, I alarmed almost every House, till I got to Lexington. I found Mess rs. Hancock & Adams at the Rev. Mr. Clark's; I told them my errand, and inquired for Mr. Samuel Dawes; they said he had not been there; I related the story of the two officers, & supposed that He must have been stopped, as he ought to have been there before me.

Revere alerts Sam Adams and John Hancock by A. L. Ripley (author's collection)

After I had been there about half an Hour, Mr. Dawes came; we refreshed ourselves, and set off for Concord, to secure the Stores, &c. there. We were overtaken by a young Doctor Samuel Prescott, whom we found to be a high Son of Liberty.

I told them of the ten officers that Mr. Richard Devens met, and that it was probable we might be stopped before we got to Concord; for I supposed that after Night, they divided themselves, and that two of them had fixed themselves in such passages as were most likely to stop any intelligence going to Concord.

I likewise mentioned, that we had better alarm all the Inhabitants till we got to Concord; the young Doctor much approved of it, and said, he would stop with either of us, for the people between that & Concord knew him, & would give more credit to what we said. We had gotten nearly half way. Mr Dawes & the Doctor Prescott stopped to alarm the people of a House: I was about one hundred Rod a head, when I saw two men, in nearly the same situation as those Officers were, near Charlestown.

I called for the Doctor Prescott & Dawes to come up; in an Instant I was surrounded by four; - they had placed themselves in a Straight Road, that inclined each way; they had taken down a pair of bars on the North side of the Road, & two of them were under a tree in the pasture. The Doctor being foremost, he came up; and we tried to get past them; but they being armed with pistols & swords, they forced us into the pasture; the Doctor jumped his Horse over a low Stone wall, and got to Concord.

I observed a Wood at a Small distance, & made for that. When I got there, out Started Six officers, on Horseback, and ordered me to dismount;-one of them, who appeared to have the command, examine me, where I came from, & what my Name Was? I told him. He asked me if I was an express? I answered in the affirmative.

He demanded what time I left Boston. I told him; and added, that their troops had catch-ed aground in passing the River, and that there would be five hundred Americans there in a short time, for I had alarmed the Country all the way up. He immediately rode towards those who stopped us, when all five of them came down upon a full gallop; One of them, whom I afterwards found to be Major Mitchel, of the 5th Regiment, Clapped his pistol to my head, called me by name, & told me he was going to ask me some questions, & if I did not give him true answers, he would blow my brains out.

He then asked me similar questions to those above. He then ordered me to mount my Horse, after searching me for arms. He then ordered them to advance,

& to lead me in front. When we got to the Road, they turned down towards Lexington. When we had got about one Mile, the Major Rode up to the officer that was leading me, & told him to give me to the Sergeant. As soon as he took me, the Major ordered him, if I attempted to run, or anybody insulted them, to blow my brains out.

Paul Revere at Lexington Common on April 19, 1775 by Monica Vachula (PRR) 2003

We rode till we got near Lexington Meeting-house, when the Militia fired a Volley of Guns, which appeared to alarm them very much. The Major inquired of me how far it was to Cambridge, and if there were Any other Road? After some consultation, the Major rode up to the Sergeant, & asked if his Horse was tired? He answered him, he was - (He was a Sergeant of Grenadiers, and had a small Horse) - then, said He, take that man's Horse.

I dismounted, & the Sergeant mounted my Horse, when they all rode towards Lexington Meeting-House. I went across the Burying-ground, & some pastures, & came to the Reverend Mr. Jonas Clarke's House, where I found Mess rs. John Hancock & Sam Adams. I told them of my treatment, & they concluded to go from (Clarke's) House towards Woburn. I went with them, & a Mr. Lowell, who was a Clerk to Mr. Hancock.

When we got to the House where they intended to stop, Mr. Lowell & I returned to Mr. Clarke's, to find what was going on. When we got there, an elderly man came in; he said he had just come from the (Buckman) Tavern, that a Man had come from Boston, who said There were no British troops coming. Mr. Lowell & myself went towards the Tavern, when we met a Man (Thaddeus Bowman) on a full gallop, who told us the Troops were coming up the (Foot of) "Rocks" (Menotomy Village now Arlington Heights).

We afterwards met another, who said They were close by. Mr. Lowell asked me to go to the Buckman Tavern with him, to a Bit a Trunk of papers belonging to Mr. Hancock. We went up Chamber; & while we were getting the Trunk, We saw the British very near (Lexington Common), upon a full March.

We hurried towards Mr. Clarke's House. On our way, We passed through the Militia. There were about 50 (actual number was 77). When we had got about 100 Yards from the Lexington Meeting House the British Troops appeared on both Sides of the Meeting-House. In their Front was an Officer on Horseback. They made a Short Halt; when I saw, & heard, a Gun fired, which appeared to be a Pistol. Then I could distinguish two Guns, & then a Continual roar of Musketry; When we made off with the Trunk.

As I have mentioned to Dr. Church, perhaps it might not be disagreeable to mention some Matters of my own knowledge, respecting Him. He appeared to be a high son of Liberty. He frequented all the places where they met, Was encouraged by all the leaders of the Sons of Liberty, & it appeared he was respected by them, though I knew that Dr. Warren did not have the greatest affection for him. He was esteemed a very capable writer, especially in verse; and as the Whig party needed every Strength, they feared, as well as courted Him.

Though it was known that some of the Liberty Songs, which we composed, were parodied by him, in favor of the British, yet none dare charge him with it. I was a constant & critical observer of him, and I must say, that I never thought of Him a man of Principle; and I doubted much in my own mind, whether He was a real Whig. I knew that He kept company with a Capt. Price, a half-pay British officer, & that He frequently dined with him, & Robinson, one of the Commissioners. I know that one of his intimate acquaintances asked him Why he was so often with Robinson and Price? His answer was that He kept Company with them on purpose to find out their plans.

The day after the Battle of Lexington, met him in Cambridge, when He showed

me some blood on his stocking, which he said splattered on him from a Man who was killed near him, as he was urging the Militia on.

I well remember, that I argued with myself, if a Man will risque his life in a Cause, he must be a Friend to that cause; & I never suspected him after, till He was

charged with being a Traitor.

The same day I met Dr. Warren. He was President of the Committee of Safety. He engaged me as a Messenger, to do the out of doors business for that committee; which gave me an opportunity of being frequently with them. The Friday evening after, about sun set, I was sitting with some, or near all that Committee, in their room, which was

at Mr. Hastings's House at Cambridge. Dr. Church, all at once, started up - Dr. Warren, said He, I am determined to go into Boston tomorrow - (it set them all a staring) - Dr. Warren replied, Are you serious, Dr. Church?

They will Hang you if they catch you in Boston. He replied, I am serious, and am determined to go on all adventures. After a considerable conversation, Dr. Warren said, If you are determined, let us make some business for you. They agreed that he should go to Bit medicine for their & our Wounded officers. He went the next morning; & I think he came back on Sunday evening. After He had told the Committee how things were,

I took him aside, & inquired particularly how they treated him? he said, that as soon as he got to their lines on Boston Neck, they made him a prisoner, & carried him to General Gage, where He was examined, & then He was sent to Gould's Barracks, & was not suffered to go home but once. After He was taken up, for holding a Correspondence with the British, I came a Cross Deacon Caleb Davis; we entered into Conversation about Him; He told me, that the morning Church went into Boston, He (Davis) received a Billet for General Gage - (he then did not know that Church was in Town). When he got to the General's House, he was told, the General could not be spoken with, that He was in private with a Gentleman; that He waited near half an Hour. When General Gage & Dr. Church came out of a Room, discoursing together, like persons who had been long acquainted.

He appeared to be quite surprised at seeing Deacon Davis there; that he (Church) went where he pleased, while in Boston, only Major Caine, one of Gage's Aids, went with him. I was told by another person whom I could depend upon, that he saw Church go into General Gage's House, at the above time; that He got out of the Chaise and went up the steps more like a Man that was acquainted, than a prisoner. Sometime after, perhaps a Year or two, I fell in company with a Gentleman who studied with Church in discoursing about him, I related what I have men stationed above; He said, He did not doubt that He was in the Interest of the British; & that it was He who informed Gen. Gage That he knew for Certain, that a Short time before the Battle of Lexington, (for He then lived with Him, & took Care of his Business & Books). He had no money by him, and was much driven for money; that all at once, He had several Hundred New British Guineas; and that He thought at the time, where they came from.

Thus, Sir, I have endeavored to give you a short detail of some matters, of which perhaps no person but myself have documents, or knowledge. I have mentioned some names which you are acquainted with: I wish you would ask them, if they can remember the circumstances I allude to.

I am, Sir, with every Sentiment of esteem, Your Humble Servant,

Paul Revere"

Paul Revere by the Mystic River by Monica Vachula Paul Revere's Ride 2003

The tragic events of April 18 and 19, 1775 inspired the Colonists to join together and fight the American Revolution against British rule. Here is a newspaper account from the Salem, Massachusetts Gazette April – May, 1775 with the Colonial perspective of what happened on April 18 – 19, 1775:

"A BLOODY BUTCHERY, BY THE BRITISH TROOPS: OR, THE RUNAWAY FIGHT OF THE REGULARS.

Being the PARTICULARS of the VICTORIOUS BATTLE fought at and near CONCORD, situated Twenty Miles from BOSTON, in the Province of the Massachusetts-Bay, in New-England, between Two Thousand Regular Troops, belonging to his Britannic Majesty, and a few Hundred Provincial Troops, belonging to the Province of Massachusetts-Bay, which lasted from Sun-rise to Sun-set on the Nineteenth of April, One Thousand Seven Hundred and Seventy-five, when it was decided greatly in favor of the latter. Part of which has never before been printed. These Particulars are now published in this Form, at the Request of the Friends to the Deceased WORTHIES, who died gloriously fighting in the CAUSE OF LIBERTY and their COUNTRY; and it is their Desire that every Householder in America, who are sincere Well-withers to the American Colonies, may be possessed of the same, either to frame and glass, or otherwise to preserve in their Houses, out only as a Token of Gratitude to the Memory of the Deceased Forty Persons, but as a perpetual Memorial of that important Event, on which perhaps, may depend the future FREEDOM and GREATNESS of the COMMON-WEALTH of AMERICA. To which is annexed, A FUNERAL ELEGY on those who were slain in the Battle. (The Second Edition was corrected with some Additions.)

From E. Russell's Salem Gazette, of Newbury and Marblehead Advertiser, published on Friday, April 21, 1775.

ON Tuesday evening the eighteenth instant, a body of soldier under the command of Lieutenant-Colonel Smith, to the amount of about eight hundred men, embarked from Barton's -Point, in Boston, about eleven o'clock, crossed Charles -River, landed at Phil's Farm, in Cambridge, and marched immediately up to Lexington, near twelve miles from Boston; at sun-rise they observing between thirty and forty inhabitants exercising near the meeting-House, the Commanding-Officer ordered them to lay down their arms and disperse, which not being directly complied with, he " damned them for a pack of rebels, " ordered his men to fire upon them, and killed eight men on the spot, besides wounding several more. The army then proceeded to Concord, drew up on the parade, near the meeting-house, during which time the inhabitants from the neighboring towns collected and took possession of the adjacent bills, about eleven o'clock the firing began on both sides, which linked near an hour, when the regular troops began to retreat, the provincials closely pursuing them to a bridge at a small distance, which the regular took up as they passed; they then renewed the fire, and same were slain on both sides; but the regulars still retreated, and the provincials pursued them down to Lexington, where the regulars, about three o'clock in the afternoon, met with a reinforcement of about twelve hundred men, commanded by Earl Percy, with two brass field pieces; they again renewed the attack upon the provincials, but soon thought proper further to retreat towards their head-quarters, the provincials pursued them into Charlestown, where they arrive about sunset; taking immediately and advantageous poll on Bunker's -Hill, about a mile from the ferry: the provincials, of the pursuit. The loss we have not been able to ascertain, but it is said about one hundred Regulars are killed and fifty wounded, among which were several officers: Two-officers and a number of soldiers were taken prisoners. On the part of the province, we hear that thirty-five were slain and several wounded. The above is as particular an account of the engagement, as can at this time be collected, in the present confused state of the province.

We hear an officer and his servant, with a pair of pistols, were yesterday taken and secured by our people, at Roxbury, on their way to Cattle William.

SALEM, APRIL 25, 1775

LAST Wednesday, the nineteenth of April, the troops of his Britannic Majesty commence hostilities upon the people of this province, attended with circumstances of cruelty not less brutal than what our venerable Ancestors received from the vile savages of the wilderness. The particulars relative to this interesting event, by which we are involved in all the horrors of a civil war, we have endeavored to collect as well as the present confused state of affairs will admit.

On Tuesday evening a detachment from the army, consisting, it is said, of eight or nine hundred men, commanded by Lieutenant-Colonel Smith, embarked at the bottom of the common at Boston, on board a number of boats, and landed at Phipps Farm, a little way up Charles -River, from whence they proceeded with silence and expedition, on their way to Concord, about eighteen miles from Boston. The people were soon alarmed, and began to assemble, in several towns, before day-light in order to watch the motion of the troops. At Lexington, six miles below Concord, a company of militia, of about one hundred men, mustered near the meeting-house; the troops came in light of them just before sun-rise; and running within a few rods of them, the Commanding-Officer accosted the militia so in words to his effect;

Lexington Common "Disperse you rebels" by A. Lassell Ripley (author's collection)

—" Disperse you rebels—Damn you, throw down your arms and disperse:" Upon which the troops huzzah, and immediately one or two officers discharged their pistols, which were instantaneously followed by the firing of four or five of the soldiers, and then there seemed to be a general discharge from the whole body: Eight of our men were killed, and nine wounded. In a few minutes after this action the enemy renewed their march for Concord; at which place they destroyed several carriages, carriage-wheels, and about twenty barrels of flour, all belonging to the province. Here about one hundred men going towards a bridge, of which the enemy were in possession, the latter fired, and killed two of our men, who then returned the fire, and obliged the enemy to retreat back to Lexington, where they met Lord Percy, with a large reinforcement, with two pieces of cannon. The enemy now having a body of about eighteen hundred men made a halt, picked up many of their dead, and took care of their wounded. At Menotomy, a few of our men, belonging to the detachment from Lynn-End, attacked a party of twelve of the enemy, (carrying stores and provisions to the troops) killed two of them, wounded several, took six prisoners, shot five horses, and took possession of all their arms, stores, provisions, &c. without any loss on our side; among those who were killed was a Lieutenant, who went with the provisions for his recreation, and to view the country, the officer of the guard who generally attends on such occasions being only a sergeant.—The enemy having halted one or two hours at Lexington, found it necessary to make a second retreat, carrying with them many of their dead and wounded, who they put in chaises and on horses that they found standing in the road. They continued their retreat from Lexington to Charlestown with great precipitation; and notwithstanding their field pieces, our people continued the pursuit, firing at them until they got to Charlestown -Neck, (which they reached a little after sunset) over which the enemy passed, proceeded up Bunker's -Hill, and soon afterwards went into the town, under the protection of the Somerset man of war of seventy-four guns.

In Lexington the enemy set fire to Deacon Joseph Loring's house and barn, Mrs. Mulliken's house and shop, and Mr. Joshua Bord's house and shop, which were all consumed. They also let fire to several other houses, but our people extinguished the flames. They pillaged almost every house they passed by, breaking and destroying doors, windows, etc. and carrying off clothing and other valuable effects. It appeared to be their design to burn and destroy all before them; and nothing but our vigorous pursuit prevented their internal purposes from being put into execution. But the savage barbarity exercised upon the bodies of our unfortunate brethren who fall, is almost incredible: Not content with shooting down the unarmed, aged, and infirm, they disregarded the cries of the wounded, killing them without mercy, and mangling their bodies in the most shocking manner.

We have the pleasure to say, that notwithstanding the highest provocations given by the enemy, not one instance of cruelty, that we have heard of, was committed by our victorious militia; but, listening to the merciful dictates of the Christian religion, they "breathed higher sentiments of humanity."

By an account of the loss of the enemy, fail to have come from an officer of one of the men of war, it appears that sixty-three of the regulars, and forty-nine marines were killed, and one hundred and three of both wounded; In all two hundred and fifteen. Lieut. Gould, of the fourth regiment who was wounded, and Lieut. Potter, of the marines, and about twelve soldiers, are prisoners.

Mr. James Howard and one of the regulars discharged their pieces at the same instant, and each killed the other.

The public most sincerely sympathize with the friends and relations of our deceased brethren, who gloriously sacrificed their lives in fighting for the liberties of their country. By their noble, intrepid conduct? in helping to defeat the forces of an ungrateful Tyrant, they have endeared their memories to the present generation who will transmit their names to poll-er with the highest honor.

The above account is to obtain. We can only add that the town of Boston is now invested by a vast army of our brave Countrymen, who have shown our assistance from all quarters. GOD grants them assistance in the extrapolation of our cruel and unnatural enemies.

SALEM, MAY 5, 1775

ON the nineteenth of April were killed, among others, by the British troops, at Menotomy, as he was courageously defending his country's rights, the good, the pious, and friendly Mr. Daniel Townsend, of Lynn-End. He was a constant and ready friend to the poor and afflicted; a good adviser in case of difficulty, and an able, mild, and sincere reprove of those who were out of the way. In short, he was a friend to his country, a blessing to society, and an ornament to the church, of which he was a member. He has left an amiable consort, and five young children, to bewail the loss.

Lie, valiant Townsend, in the peaceful shades.—We trust Immortal honors mingle with thy dust.

What! tho' thy body struggled in the gore; So did thy Savior's body long before! And as he raised his own, by power divine; So the same power shall also quicken thine, And in eternal glory, mayst thou shine.

On Thursday the twentieth past, the bodies of eleven of the unfortunate persons who fell in the Battle were collected together and buried at Medford.

And on Friday the bodies of Messieurs Henry Jacobs, Samuel Code, Ebenezer Goldthwait, George Southwick, Benjamin Daland Jr., Jotham Webb, and Perley Putnam, of Danvers, who were likewise slain fighting in the GLORIOUS CAUSE OF LIBERTY AND THEIR COUNTRY, on the nineteenth of April, were respectfully interred among their friends in the different parishes belonging to that town, their corpse being attended to the place of interment by two companion of minute-men from this place, and a large concourse of people from this and the neighboring towns; previous to their interment, an excellent and well-adapted prayer was delivered by the Reverend Mr. Holt, of that place.

Same day the remains of Messieurs Asahel Porter and Daniel Thompson, of Woburn, who also fell victims to tyranny, were decently interred at that place, attended to the grave by a multitude of persons who assembled on the occasion from that and the neighboring towns: Before they were interred, a very suitable sermon and prayer was delivered by the Reverend Mr. Sherman.

Lieutenant Joseph Knight, of the fifth Regiment died at Boston the next day after the engagement, of his wounds he received-in the same. He was greatly regretted, being esteemed one of the best officers among the King's troops.

Lieut. Hall, of the regulars, died of his wounds on Wednesday last at the provincial hospital: His remains were the next day conveyed to Charlestown, attended by a company of provincials, and several officers of distinction, and there delivered to the order of General Gage. Twenty-three wounded soldiers later died from the Battle.

Lieutenant Hawkshaw was wounded in the check, and it is thought that he will not recover. Lieutenant Gere was wounded in the arm: About 12 other officers are wounded.

We can assure the public, from the best authority, that our brethren, of all the colonies which we can yet have heard from, are firm and unshaken in their attachment to the common cause of America; and that they are now ready, with their lives and fortunes, to assist us in defeating and cruel designs of our implacable enemies.

We have received no particulars of the transactions between General Gage and the inhabitants of Boston. It is certain that the people have delivered up their arms; very few of them have, however, been permitted to leave the town, notwithstanding the promise of the General."

General Henry Knox Trail Framingham, MA (Wikimedia Commons Public Domain)

Knox's Nobel Train of Artillery (US National Archives Public Domain)

KNOX'S LEGENDARY ACHIEVEMENT

General Washington after taking command at Cambridge, Massachusetts befriended Boston native Henry Knox, and sent him on a secret mission. Knox went to Fort Ticonderoga in New York to bring back a train of artillery to place them on Dorchester Heights in Boston. Washington promoted Knox to General of his artillery.

The path Knox's men took dragging 58 cannons with oxen and winter sleds is now called the Henry Knox Trail. Some of Henry Knox's trail is on the map in this book. Knox's Noble Train of Artillery went east through the Western Massachusetts communities, then the cities of Worcester, Framingham, Sudbury, Wayland, Weston, Waltham, Watertown, Cambridge, Roxbury, South Boston to Dorchester Heights. There is a series of marker stones from New York across Massachusetts marking this historic trail that is a completely amazing achievement in the annals of military history.

Washington's plan worked, and the British evacuated the city on their ships of war, and traveled north to Halifax, Nova Scotia, Canada to resupply and reorganize. The war had just begun, and would not officially end until the Treaty of Paris in 1783.

All this history traveling about, and research made Riley very tired (photo by author)

THE TREASURE IS OUT THERE WAITING

I have had many troubles in life, so I write splendid treasure tales. Somewhere along all these Cities, Towns, great historical places, routes of travel, Battle Roads, important people lived here, traveled past here, or fought here during 1770 to 1776.

The treasure is hidden very well. No one will just happen upon it. You really need to read the book multiple times to get into the chase. Then go have safe fun with your family, friends, youth organizations, or Scouts Program.

If you find the treasure, very discreetly and quietly take it. Please do not draw attention to yourself. If you found my pirate's treasure, in honor of my friend Forrest Fenn, "I give you the title to it." Follow the contact instructions in the treasure chest to receive another nice finder's reward. This way, we can publicly let folks know if *Riley's Treasure Chase* has officially ended.

Perhaps you didn't find it yet because the treasure search area that you must search is pretty large, so don't get easily frustrated or discouraged. No one said the treasure would be easy to find. No challenge would equal no fun. It will take time, and effort for the finder to locate the chest. The great challenge makes the quest more worthy. I can't promise you will find treasure, but I can imagine you keeping a positive attitude and enjoying this treasure chase.

THE TRUE TREASURE

The true treasure is in spending time with your family, loved ones and friends. I hope you had fun on the treasure hunt or chase. If so, please tell others to get a book so they can enjoy the same great experiences that your family and friends had.

Maybe with your parents approval upload your videos on social media or photos on Facebook, etc. so others can enjoy your group's efforts. Please help me spread the word about my treasure hunts. I want folks to have fun and will be making oversize maps that will be sold to better help searchers plan their treasure hunts.

I'm not a rich man. I had to work hard at an hourly rate to earn the money. Then I hid more than $100,000 worth of treasure between my first two books: *Lady Liberty's Treasure Hunt* and *Riley's Treasure Chase*. Thank heaven my wife Laurel is patient and kind. She and I want you to have fun.

Over time, I believe the value of these treasures may double, like that of Forrest Finn's initial $600,000 value treasure, which sold by piece at Heritage Auctions Texas for over 1.2 million dollars in 2023. I know how valuable Forrest Fenn's Treasure was because I bought seven of his coins, and other pieces of his treasure. The British Golden Hare treasure from the *Masquerade* book sold for an exuberant amount as well.

PERHAPS DOCUMENT YOUR FUN TREASURE HUNTS ON YOUR PARENT'S SOCIAL MEDIA ACCOUNTS

Please help to spread the word so folks buy my books; and then go off on great adventures in the spring, summer, or fall months and closely study the seasons of America's past. I believe it's very important to teach children history, and to get them out in nature.

My books are less expensive than attending a Red Sox, Patriots, Bruins, Celtics, Revolution, Harvard University, Boston College, Boston University, or Northeastern University athletic event. I have attended all of them, and I hope you attend a game when you're in town. Boston sports teams are legendary, and their fans are great too. It's a really great place to live or attend college!

Parents, please help your children to safely enjoy these great adventures but let them win the treasure prize themselves. It's better for the children to earn achievements on their own, as Scouting has been teaching us for the past century.

My best dog friend Riley was there when the Bay State Pirate made his mark upon this world by hiding his great treasure. Any child will smile with pride, and joy when they look upon *Riley's Treasure Chase* treasure chest contents. There is a special note inside that treasure chest for the finder. Please follow those finder instructions carefully.

Riley's Treasure Chase is not the same as *Lady Liberty's Treasure Hunt*. However, they are companion books in that both serve as mechanisms to teach others American History in a fun way. They also overlap a little in the writing and in the Bay State since *Riley's Treasure Chase* was born of *Lady Liberty's Treasure Hunt*. Riley's book was adapted from Lady Liberty's book to be more helpful to the younger readers, and with fewer adult themes related to loss.

Too many folks have been bored or dulled to our great American history, so it's time to make it fun again! That is the educational purpose of this book, and *Lady Liberty's Treasure Hunt*, too.

CONCLUDING THOUGHTS

It is best to watch the Boston Marathon on the evening news because the alarm riders did not come from Hopkinton on that overnight into the morning on Patriot's Day. The Boston Marathon is great, but I wish they ran it in October so folks could celebrate Patriot's Day properly in all the places that participated in the American Revolution on April 18 and 19, 1775.

Monuments and granite historical markers stand so we never forget their immortal glory. Take a picture at these historic places with your family or friends so you can remember your great treasure chase journeys in the years ahead.

Please plan ahead and perhaps go to Patriot's Day Weekend Battle Reenactments at Lexington Common, Old North Bridge Concord, Minuteman National Park Battle Road: Meriam's Corner, Hartwell Tavern, Parker's Revenge, Munroe Tavern Lexington toward East Lexington, and Jason Russell House Arlington Center (formerly Menotomy). Let's keep the Spirit of '75 alive, long after 2025. The American Revolution did not end until 1783, when the liberty bell rang.

If you come to visit New England during the Autumn colors, The Powder House Alarm Reenactment is September 1 on Quarry Hill Somerville, and the Sudbury Minutemen fight His Majesty's 10th Regiment of Foot every October by Longfellow's Historic Wayside Inn (formerly called Howe's or Red Horse Tavern). These are all wonderful events, if the weather is good. This is New England, so please check the weather carefully.

It's how we overcome our struggles that define us in life. The same can be said for our nation. By overcoming its struggles, a nation lit the lanterns, then the light of *Lady Liberty's* torch. A gift from our great ally France. As you know, I wrote another book called *Lady Liberty's Treasure Hunt* with the beautiful lady on the cover.

We all know that young William Diamond stood bravely on that cool, breezy morning with his drum, following the orders from his Captain.

Perhaps attend the Patriot's Day Concord, Lexington and Arlington parades or Fife and Drum musters as I have so many times before and listen to the beautiful music of the Old Guard, William Diamond's Corp or of the Middlesex County Volunteers, and others as they remember yesteryear. You will not be disappointed. My Aunt Marion (O'Connell) Dolan loved those Fife and Drum Tattoos. We went to as many as we could.

Berton Bradley explained it well in his poem:

"Listen, my children, and you shall hear Of a lovely feminine Paul Revere Who rode an equally famous ride Through a different part of the (dangerous) countryside, Where Sybil Ludington's name recalls A ride as (brave and) daring as Paul's."

Patriot Sybil Ludington (age 16) made her brave night journey across 40 miles of New York and Connecticut in the pouring rain, across muddy roads and farmlands, to alert her father Colonel Henry Ludington's militia to wake on April 26, 1777. New York and Connecticut are part of *Lady Liberty's Treasure Hunt* but not *Riley's Treasure Chase*. To be successful, you must follow her example by remembering the spirits of '75 in the Bay State.

What were the times and routes of travel of Paul Revere, William Dawes, and Dr. Samuel Prescott? Their route areas are in play. All the alarm riders were important and known as "Sons of Liberty."

Check those blue arrows on the map closely. What route of march did they take to go fight at Concord, Lincoln, Lexington, Menotomy Village (Arlington), Cambridge, Mystic Village (Medford), Somerville, and Charlestown (Boston)?

The three British leaders' routes of travel in red from Boston to Concord and back again are also in play. You can be right or wrong by either walking too far or not far enough. The British learned this by a rude bridge.

Captain Parker's home was on Spring Street near the Waltham line, but his likeness stands forevermore under the shadow of the Stars and Stripes.

The Minutemen and Militia received the alarm. All of them left their families and farms to defend their rights. Amos Doolittle, Henry Sandham, Aiden Lassell Ripley, Don Troiani, Harry Jaeck, Cortney Skinner, Mort Kunstler, Cyrus Dallin, and Daniel Chester French remember them all in their great works.

So many communities have built beautiful memorial sculptures or granite markers along their lines of march to rightly remember their Patriots. Make sure you salute them all, as the Scouts do, when they pass by each Patriot's Day weekend on these historic lines of march.

Colonel William Prescott at Bunker Hill Charlestown 1775 (NPS Public Domain)

No one town or city stood alone or did all the fighting. All equally deserve credit for answering Liberty's call. So any town or city that sent Minutemen, Militia, or alarm riders out—their routes of travel to the battle areas are in play, including in their own communities. Ask your local Minutemen or Militia for information about this.

The Daughters of the American Revolution, Scouting organizations, and local Historical Society groups may help you, too. Not one of them alone, but all of them together matter a great deal, like their ancestors before them.

A pirate makes his mark upon this world. His time on this earth may be fleeting, but he did it his way.

My mapmaker did wonderful work. When asked if I would leave an X on the maps to mark where the pirate left treasure, I responded: "If they find the pirate's mark, I give them the title to that chest." This is in honor of my friend Forrest Fenn who used similar words in his *The Thrill of the Chase* treasure hunt.

The full moon rose before the glorious morning. Unless you are very wise, Riley's Chase's treasure lies forever under peaceful, starry skies.

The Massachusetts Minutemen, and Militia took this solemn oath in 1774 or 1775:

"We trust in God, that should that state of our affairs require it, we shall be ready to sacrifice our estates and every thing dear in life itself, in support of the common cause."

Please remember our brave Patriots who died as a result of Battle on April 19, 1775:

Name:	Town From:	Where killed:	Where Buried:
Robert Munroe	Lexington	Lexington Common	Lexington Common
Jonas Parker	Lexington	Lexington Common	Lexington Common
Jonathan Harrington	Lexington	Lexington Common	Lexington Common
Caleb Harrington***	Lexington	Lexington Common	Lexington Common
Samuel Hadley	Lexington	Lexington Common	Lexington Common
John Brown	Lexington	Lexington Common	Lexington Common
Asahel Porter*	Woburn	in Lexington Center	Woburn
Abel Prescott Jr.**	Concord	mortal wound Concord	Unknown Concord
Captain Isaac Davis	Acton	North Bridge Concord	Acton Center
Abner Hosner	Acton	North Bridge Concord	Acton Center
Capt Jonathan Wilson	Bedford	Near Elm Brook Lincoln	Bedford
Daniel Thompson	Woburn	Brooks Tavern Lincoln	Woburn
Nathaniel Wyman	Lexington	Brooks Tavern Lincoln	Lexington Center
Asahel Reed	Sudbury	Hartwell Tavern Lincoln	Sudbury Center
James Hayward	Acton	Lexington Acton	Fiske Farm Center
Josiah Haynes	Sudbury	Concord Hill Lexington	Sudbury Center
Jedediah Munroe	Lexington	Lexington	Lexington Center
John Raymond*	Lexington	Munroe Tavern Lexington	Lexington
Joseph Coolidge	Watertown	East Lexington/Menotomy	Watertown
Henry Jacobs	Danvers	Russell House Menotomy	Danvers
Samuel Cook	Danvers	Russell House Menotomy	Danvers
Ebenezer Goldthwait	Danvers	Russell House Menotomy	Danvers
George Southwick	Danvers	Russell House Menotomy	Danvers
Benjamin Daland	Danvers	Russell House Menotomy	Danvers
Jothan Webb	Danvers	Russell House Menotomy	Danvers
Perley Putnam	Danvers	Russell House Menotomy	Danvers
Daniel Townsend	Lynn	Russell House Menotomy	Lynnfield
Reuben Kennison	Beverly	Russell House Menotomy	Danvers
William Flint	Lynn	Russell House Menotomy	Arlington
Thomas Hadley	Lynn	Russell House Menotomy	Arlington
Jason Russell	Arlington	Russell House Menotomy	Arlington
William Polly	Medford	By Mill Pond Menotomy	Medford

Henry Putnam	Medford	By Meeting House Menotomy	Medford
Benjamin Pierce	Salem	By Meeting House Menotomy	Arlington
Lieutenant John Bacon	Needham	By Meeting House Menotomy	Arlington
Sergeant Elisha Mills	Needham	By Meeting House Menotomy	Arlington
Amos Mills	Needham	By Meeting House Menotomy	Arlington
Nathaniel Chamberlain	Needham	By Meeting House Menotomy	Arlington
Jonathon Parker	Dedham	By Meeting House Menotomy	Arlington
Elias Haven	Dover	By Meeting House Menotomy	Arlington
Abednego Ramsdell	Lynn	By Meeting House Menotomy	Arlington
Jabez Wyman	Arlington	In Cooper Tavern Menotomy	Arlington
Jason Winship	Arlington	In Cooper Tavern Menotomy	Arlington
Moses Richardson	Cambridge	Watkin's Corner Cambridge	Cambridge
John Hicks	Cambridge	Watkin's Corner Cambridge	Cambridge
William Marcy	Cambridge	Watkin's Corner Cambridge	Cambridge
Major Isaac Gardner	Brookline	Watkin's Corner Cambridge	Brookline
James Miller	Somerville	Prospect Hill Somerville	Unknown
Edward Barber*	Charlestown	Charlestown Neck	Charlestown

*Unarmed tragic casualty of war shot by British Troops April 19, 1775

**Sons of Liberty Warning Rider shot in the side by the British Soldier April 19 and later died of dysentery from his battle wound in September 1775.

*** 24 year old guarding the powder on the second floor of the Meeting House. He got frightened when surrounded by the British all all sides of the building, and fled on foot away from the British when he was shot. It is unclear if he was armed or not.

Many Minutemen and Militia Companies had wounded, and missing men on April 19, 1775:

Acton - Wounded: Luther Blanchard of Littleton (Boxborough), and Ezekiel Davis

Arlington (Menotomy Village West Cambridge) - Wounded: Samuel Whittemore

Bedford - Wounded: Job Lane

Beverly - Wounded: Nathaniel Cleaves, William Dodge III, and Samuel Woodbury

Billerica - Wounded: Timothy Blanchard, and John Nichols

Concord - Captain Nathan Barrett, Captain Charles Miles, Captain George Minot, and Jonas Brown. There is a Monument dedicated to him on Monument St. Concord near the Carlisle town line it says: "He was wounded at the North Bridge, bleeding he chased the enemy nine miles."

Chelmsford - Wounded; Oliver Barron, and Aaron Chamberlain.

Danvers - Wounded: Nathan Putnam & Dennison Wallis. Missing: Joseph Bell.

Dedham - Wounded: Israel Everett.

Framingham - Wounded: Daniel Hemenway.

Lexington: Wounded: Francis Brown, Joseph Comee, Prince Estrabrook, Nathaniel Farmer, Solomon Pierce, John Robbins, John Tidd and Thomas Winship.

Lincoln - Wounded; Joshua Brooks.

Needham - Wounded: Eleazer Kingsbury, and John Tolman.

Newton - Wounded: Noah Wiswell.

Stow (Maynard Village of Town) - Wounded: Daniel Conant.

Stoneham - Wounded: Edward Bucknam Jr.

Woburn - Jacob Bacon, (Unknown First Name) Johnson, and George Reed.

"They poured out their generous blood like water, before they knew whether it would fertilize the land of freedom or of bondage (Daniel Webster at Bunker Hill Boston Monument First Oration 1825)."

While They Sleep

by Michael Cloherty O'Connell

(Inspired by Billerica, Massachusetts native Leonard Buckland)

Farmer's meadows, and fields where wild flowers and crops now grow;
And in pine scented woods and peaceful hollows, thick with shade.
They fought the King's bold crimson troops; face to face,
And their courage did not fade.

There were many brave Minutemen and Militia Companies from Middlesex,
Essex, Suffolk, and Norfolk Counties that answered the alarm.
And for some of those brave men; they would never come home,
To tell of the fife, rattle of the drums or battle on that sad but glorious day.
They fought and bled for hearth, home, family and the land they loved
With courage, honor and a reverence for God.

And when the count was known: fifty were killed, forty wounded and five missing from that day's horrible
    costs for liberty's sake.
Likewise the British, Irish, Scottish, Welsh, and Loyalist's wives would all feel
Great sorrow for 73 were dead, 174 wounded, and 26 missing trying to keep the Massachusetts Bay
    Colony for King George III on the morrow.
Bless all their souls in scattered graves across those Battle Road Towns,
For they died for a British or Colonial cause they believed in.

It does not now matter who was right or wrong, or who fired first?
Their anger, thirst, revenge, hardship and suffering is now well known.
May they they rest in peace in those quiet places of permanent sleep,
That still hear the echo of past musket fire or the roar of cannon every April
Their fight is long over but we remember them, and honor them still;
May they rest in their silent peaceful slumber of their sleep, while we weep.

I randomly placed valuables and collectibles in *Riley's Treasure* and *Lady Liberty's Treasure.* The adult treasure hunt is more difficult to find so that prize is more valuable than the youth reader's treasure.

The below listed items; that I collected over my lifetime; are worth over $100,000 US dollars in 2024, and are physically out there in treasure chests for someone to locate them in the years ahead:

British Silver The Royal Celebration 10 OZ. .999 Silver Bars

Archangel Michael 10 OZ .999 Silver Bars

Rare 1947 Seal 50 Cent piece

(2) France Napoleon 1 rare 1 Decime 1814

France Napoleon 1813 Silver Coin

France 1580 Henry III Double Sol Parisis Silver

English King Henry III Medieval 1216 – 1272 A.D.

(2) Medieval England Henry VIII First Coinage

US 1910 Gold $10 Indian Head Eagle

US 1908 Gold $10 Indian Head Eagle

US Gold $5 Indian Head

US Gold $2.5 Indian Head

France 1583 Silver Double Sol Parisis Henry III

France 2020 Silver $10 Euro Lafayette to Boston

Colonial Spanish 1400's Silver Cob Pirate Coins

Colonial Spanish 1600's Pirate Shipwreck Cob Coins

Spanish 1869 – 1890 5 Cent pieces

Spanish Mid 1840's – 1860 coins

Spanish 1820 – 1840 Maravedis coins

Spanish 1800 – 1820 Maravedis coins

Spanish 1700 – 1799 Maravedis coins

Spanish 1600's Pirate Cobs

Spanish Shipwreck 1826 Pirate Coin Real

Numerous US Buffalo Head Nickels

Numerous US Silver Peace Dollars

Numerous US Silver Morgan Dollars

US Eisenhower Bicentennial Silver dollars

1976 US Kennedy Half Dollars

US 1975 - 1976 Bicentennial Quarters

Irish Connemara Marble Jewelry

1700's Colonial Powder Horns

1885 Stanley London reproduction compass

Old style reproduction telescope

Original US Civil War Era Cavalry or Officers Telescope

Several Forrest Fenn *The Thrill of the Chase* treasure chest treasure coins

Several Forrest Fenn *The Thrill of the Chase* treasure relic pieces

US Grant Bronze Medals (US copies of 1863 original bronze medals)

1826 Spanish Colonial Shipwreck Pirate Coin

1788 Spanish Colonial Pirate Shipwreck Coin

1808 Spanish Pirate Shipwreck Coin

1746 Spanish Pirate Coin

1825 Spanish Pirate Coin

Sterling Silver Bunker & Breed's Hill Boston Spoon

Sterling Silver Old North Church Boston Spoon

Rare 1825 Spanish Pirate Coin

Multiple 1870 Spanish Colonial Shipwreck Coins

1798 Spanish Colonial Shipwreck Pirate Coin

1600's Spanish Pirate Cob Coin

1987 France Lafayette Silver Coin

2020 France Euro Lafayette Silver 2 OZ. Coin

1847 Spanish Pirate Coin

1861 Spanish 1861 Pirate Coin

1840 Spanish Pirate Shipwreck Coins

Rare Roman Trajan Decius Silver Antoninus Coin

Rare Roman Empire Augustus Spanish Mint LLerda Coin

1802 Spanish ½ Reale Pirate Golden Era Coin

1778 Spanish Colonial ½ Reale Golden Era Pirate Coin

Rare 1700's Crusaders Spanish ½ Reale Segovia Coin

Rare 12th Century Crusaders Spanish ½ Reale Coin

Rare 1200's Medieval Spanish Coin

Rare 1600's Spanish Colonial Coin

1829 Spanish Shipwreck Pirate Coin

1868 Spanish Shipwreck Pirate Coin

1775 Spanish ½ Reale Charles III Colonial Coin

Pre-Columbian Frog Style Jewelry Modern Pieces

Many NGC Rare & Precious Coin Slabs

1857 US $1 Gold Coins

1900 US Lafayette Commemorative Silver Dollars

US President Franklin Pierce (NH) Gold Coin

Rare Forrest Fenn *The Thrill of the Chase* Treasure Gold pieces

1775 Ireland/British Half Penny

1778 France Louis XVI Era Coins

1775 British King George III Half Penny

1775 British King George III North Wales Coin

Multiple 1775 – 1776 Hibernia Ireland British Half Pennies

Multiple 1775 English King George III Farthing Coins

Multiple Atocha Silver Pieces

Multiple Paul Revere's Ride ½ Troy OZ Silver Rounds

US Mint Medal General Nathaniel Greene

Stainless Steel Pirates Cross & Bones Necklaces

Paul Revere's Ride Medals

Battle of Concord Bronze Medals

1925 Lexington-Concord Sesquicentennial Silver Half Dollars

Bicentennial Paul Revere Medals

1925 US Commemorative Half Dollar

1976 Minuteman Monument Bronze Medal

2021 US General Washington Battle of Trenton Coins

Carlisle Minutemen Route to Concord Bronze Medal

.999 Silver The Birth of the Nation Lexington & Concord Rounds

Battle of Lexington and Concord Medals

Bicentennial Warning Riders Token Medal

Lexington & Concord Bicentennial Token Medals

Lexington "What a Glorious Morning" Medal

1930's Black Ruthenium 24K Buffalo Coins

US Gold Plated Buffalo Nickels

1976 Gold Plated JFK Half Dollars

US 1965 Silver Half Dollars (in honor of Laurel's year of birth)

US 1963 Silver Franklin Half Dollars (in honor of the Author's birth year)

1946 Silver Walking Half Dollar

1976 US Mint Proof Coin Sets

1976 Philadelphia Bicentennial Quarters

1976 General Stark Bicentennial Bronze Medals

US Civil War Medals

US Civil War Artist Don Troiani Rare Cased Coin

1812 US Bust Half Dollars

1812 France Napoleon .90 Silver Coin

Civil War Era Powder Flasks

American Revolution Dropped Bullet & US Civil War Relic Bullets

State of Liberty Centennial .925 Sterling Silver Token

Extremely Important Historical Figures rare written words with COA's

Various Rare Historic Tokens, Medals, Coins and Other Collectibles

Extremely Valuable .925 Sterling Silver 15 Oz Pirate Skull Statue Artwork

American Revolution US or British Dropped Bullet & US Civil War bullets

Rare Forrest Fenn style Wyoming Jade "Slick" Necklace to bring you good luck

US .999 Pure Silver Buffalo Silver Round

Extremely Rare "Fairmont Collection" US $5 Gold Liberty Coins

There is also an undisclosed amount of a Finder's Reward, if you carefully follow the written instructions inside the chest after finding a *Lady Liberty's Treasure Hunt* or *Riley's Treasure Chase* treasure.

THANK YOU AND BEST OF LUCK

Thank you for reading this book and recommending my works to others. If my books are well received; and I somehow find the time, further similar works may follow in this series.

I would love to visit your communities to do a talk and sign books or posters. Maybe you can invite me to meet a group of folks in your community, and teach me about the history of your town? I would love to meet you all, and learn more about your communities.

Be well, be happy, be safe, stay positive, and please have fun. Go well in the years ahead, my friends in history. Well now, I go. How beautiful life is.

The treasure awaits you under a full moon...

FURTHER READING:

Masquerade by Kit Williams (his treasure was already found beside King Henry XIII's first wives Catherine of Aragon Cross at Ampthill, Bedfordshire, England)

The Secret by Byron Preiss (some of his treasures are still out there to be found)

The Thrill of the Chase by Forrest Fenn (his Wyoming treasure was already located)

The Nineteenth of April, 1775 by Harold Murdock

History of the Battle of Lexington on the Morning of the 19th of April, 1775 by Elias Phinney

Redcoats and Rebels: The American Revolution Through British Eyes by Christopher Hibbert

Rise to Rebellion by Jeff Shaara

Toward Lexington by John Shy

Cyrus E. Dallin Let Justice Be Done by Rell G. Francis

History of the Town of Arlington by Benjamin Cutter

Paul Revere's Ride by David Hackett Fischer

Paul Revere, 1775 - 1818, Events of his Life by (artist A. Lassell Ripley) and Worcester Art Museum

April Morning by Howard Fast

Chaplain of the Revolution by Edward Waldo Emerson

Heroine of The Battle Road: Mary Flint Hartwell by Palmer Faran

Fighting Frigate by Edward B. Hungerford

Johnny Tremain by Esther Forbes

The Legend of Sleepy Hollow (New York) by Washington Irving

Henry Knox: Visionary General of American Revolution by Mark Puls

Amos Doolittle Engraver of the New Republic by Donald O'Brien

The Bedford Flag Unfurled by Sharon Lawrence McDonald

The Routes to and from Concord by John Bell

Life in the Woods by Henry David Thoreau

Nature by Ralph Waldo Emerson

Little Women by Louisa May Alcott

The House of Seven Gables by Nathaniel Hawthorne

Monument Man by Harold Holzer

Lady Liberty's Treasure Hunt by Michael Cloherty O'Connell (between my first two books there is over $100,000 of treasures to be located)

For adults who have remained young at heart (photograph by author)

Carpe Diem
MMXXV

ACKNOWLEDGEMENTS

I wish to thank author and historian Andrew MacAleer for his advise regarding my two books. His knowledge of American history, and insights help me give these projects better focus.

I would also like to thank my cover artist and interior designer of my books Megan Katsanevakis. Her artwork and skill on my front and back covers is amazing.

My close friend Jason Webber helped me to build my websites, and blogs. He has been so generous with his time and knowledge. I would have been completely lost without his help.

Further, I would like to thank my wife Laurel, our children, extended family and friends for putting up with the writing, researching, traveling, and not having enough time for much else. I truly hope I did not inconvenience anyone too much in this process, and apologize if I did.

Additionally, I would like to thank all the historical societies, National Park Service, and all the artists in my books. I hope you enjoy and support their art, sites, music, books, and missions in the years ahead. It takes all of us working together to make a difference.

Lastly, I want thank all you great folks that are reading this. I hope you can smile and then head off treasure hunting with your family, and friends. I hope these books made a small but positive difference in your lives. We all seek to be that pebble that hits the still pond; in that, our small efforts ripple across time.

ABOUT THE AUTHOR

American Revolutionary War and United States Civil War Historian Michael Cloherty O'Connell's career in public service spans more than four decades. He was born in Arlington; and grew up in Historic East Lexington near the First Blow for Liberty, and the Shot heard Round the World. He graduated from Lexington High School then earned a Bachelor's Degree at Northeastern University, Master's Degrees from Boston University, and Boston College. The author still lives in the Boston suburbs; with his beautiful wife Laurel, and is the proud father of four children. Michael has been actively involved in Scouting, coaching sports, and other positive youth activities all of his teenage, and adult life.